TREES
OF KRUGER

Braam van Wyk
Piet van Wyk †

Published by Struik Nature
(an imprint of Penguin Random House
South Africa (Pty) Ltd)
Reg. No. 1953/000441/07
The Estuaries No. 4, Oxbow Crescent,
Century Avenue, Century City, 7441
PO Box 1144, Cape Town, 8000
South Africa

Visit **www.penguinrandomhouse.co.za**
and join the Struik Nature Club for updates,
news, events and special offers.

First published in 2023

10 9 8 7 6 5 4 3 2 1

Publisher: Pippa Parker
Managing editor: Roelien Theron
Editor: Natalie Bell
Designer: Gillian Black
Cartographer: Nicholas De Kock,
  Geospatial Information Services unit,
  University of Pretoria
Proofreader: Emsie du Plessis

Reproduction by Studio Repro
Printed and bound in China by Toppan
Leefung Packaging and Printing
(Dongguan) Co., Ltd.

ISBN 978 1 77584 817 2 (Print)
ISBN 978 1 77584 818 9 (ePub)

Front cover: Elephants leaving the cool shade of a marula tree.
Back cover: Baobab in Kruger (main photograph); sicklebush inflorescence
(top right); bushveld-saffron fruit and leaves (bottom right).
Title page: Mopane tree.
Contents page (clockwise, from top left): Kruger scene; baobab;
large-leaved false-thorn; leadwood tree with nests of Red-billed Buffalo
Weaver, and a herd of elephant; large-leaved rock fig; buffalo crossing
a river in Kruger.

Contents

Mature marula tree; the fruit (on female trees only) are widely utilised as food as they ripen on the ground and are accessible to a wide range of animals.

Trees of Kruger

This book describes and illustrates 80 of the larger, more conspicuous and common tree species that you may see on your travels in the Kruger National Park. The aim is to help you make accurate identifications of these majestic plants.

Each tree species is showcased over two pages, combining photographs of the most representative features with concise text descriptions that use minimal botanical jargon.

Many tree identification books require access to and contact with the plant itself, but obviously this is not possible in the Park, as much of the time you will be viewing trees and wildlife from the safety of a vehicle. So these tree accounts focus on distinctive details that are visible either with the naked eye – often from a distance – or through a pair of binoculars.

Many of the tree species in Kruger (including some of the rarer ones) also occur in the rest camps, either naturally or because they were planted there, but those trees are more likely to have ID tags, removing the need for guesswork.

Trees, animals and habitat

Most Kruger visitors come to the Park to see animals and marvel at their behaviour and diversity, but let's not forget the ever-present vegetation, without which no animals would survive. Plants play a vital role in the existence of larger land animals, not only as a source of food, but also because they provide a suitable habitat for wildlife.

Unlike the mobile animals, however, the vegetation is a stationary roleplayer in the wildlife's natural territory. From grassland to savanna or forest, plants have a diversity of growth forms and occur in varying combinations, forming unique habitats.

In spite of their seemingly immobile nature (they do in fact 'move' when entering a seed phase), members of the plant kingdom have evolved to have complex forms of reproduction, communication and information processing, with each species displaying distinctive behavioural patterns.

A knowledge of members of the plant kingdom can be as intriguing and enriching – if not more – as familiarity with the furry or feathered creatures that make the Park their home. Whether these animals show up or not, the trees and shrubs are always there.

Identifying a tree is not only a challenge, it is also essential, because a name is the key to accessing information about each species.

Magnificent stand of moisture-loving fevertrees in the Pafuri area in the northern part of Kruger, with visiting elephants.

Bushveld

Broadly, the Kruger National Park's vegetation is classified as savanna, or bushveld as it is known colloquially. In simple terms, bushveld can be described as a grassland interspersed with trees. Ecologists Bob Scholes and Brian Walker portrayed it elegantly in 1993: 'Although it may have abundant grass, the bushveld does not seem to be a grassland, because it has so many trees; yet the trees are not sufficiently dense and tall to be called a forest'.

The bushveld vegetation type is primarily determined by the climate, which encompasses temperature, rainfall and fire; it is also shaped by interactions with living organisms – the 'ecosystem engineers'– prime examples of which are the elephants at the larger end of the scale and termites at the smaller.

Trees play a crucial ecological role in bushveld. Not only do they provide food, habitat and shelter for myriad animals, they also have a positive influence on soil fertility and air quality. Trees are, indeed, the 'lifeblood' of the bushveld.

Tall knob thorns and giraffe. These animals feed almost exclusively on leaves and shoots of trees, but they also favour flowers and fruit when available.

Tree diversity and fire

The Kruger National Park has a rich plant diversity of almost 2 000 species. Of these, about 400 species are trees and shrubs – but when does a shrub become a tree? There is no exact turning point – although nearly 200 woody species in the Park can reach a size that suggests they are trees, most only make it to the size of shrubs, depending on external conditions.

Regular fires are a natural and essential phenomenon in the bushveld, and result in many 'proper trees' being maintained as multi-stemmed shrubs for years, if not indefinitely. Fire is necessary to keep the woody plants in check, thereby ensuring that enough sunlight reaches the grasses and other smaller plants below.

The Park implements a sophisticated fire management programme to control vegetation composition and density. Fire suppression in bushveld leads to an increase in woody plants, a phenomenon known as bush encroachment, which results in bushveld being transformed into an impenetrable thicket, a different type of habitat unsuitable for many bushveld plants and animals. Therefore, when driving around in the Park, remember that fire-damaged, partly dead or stunted trees are part of the natural state, in contrast to the idealised picture that many people have of what the bushveld should look like.

In some parts of South Africa outside the Park – including some conservation areas – well-intended but misguided fire suppression and other inappropriate management practices have already transformed the bushveld into a superficially lush but highly unnatural state.

Controlled dry-season fire in Kruger, with marula trees in the foreground.

Tree distribution and Kruger landscapes

Because trees are rooted in the ground, the distribution of each species is strongly influenced by the substrate in which it grows, notably the underlying geology of the area (see **Map 1** opposite), but also soil type, rockiness, topography and the availability of moisture.

The tree species in this book are organised in four groups, roughly according to where they may be found and their preference for a particular substrate (see also **Guide to the species accounts**, page 28).

For the purposes of this book, the vegetation in the Park has been delineated into 35 'landscapes' (see **Map 2** overleaf, and enlargements, pages 12–17), which are based on the specific geomorphology, macroclimate, soil and vegetation pattern, and associated animal diversity (defined by Willem Gertenbach in 1983). The landscapes are numbered and shaded on the maps. A checklist of commonly found trees that occur within each landscape type is provided on pages 18–25 (with abundant or most conspicuous trees given in bold). Tree enthusiasts can use this checklist, together with the enlarged landscape maps, to identify which trees they are likely to see in the area through which they are travelling.

Typical bushveld vegetation in Kruger, with taller trees mainly along banks of rivers.

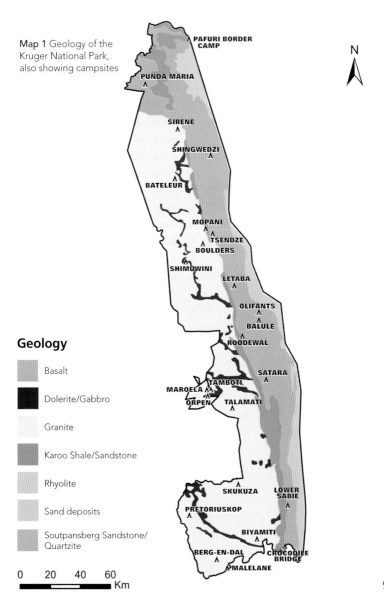

Map 1 Geology of the Kruger National Park, also showing campsites

N

PAFURI BORDER CAMP
∧

PUNDA MARIA
∧

SIRENE
∧

SHINGWEDZI
∧

BATELEUR
∧

MOPANI
∧

TSENDZE
∧

BOULDERS
∧

SHIMUWINI
∧

LETABA
∧

OLIFANTS
∧

BALULE
∧

ROODEWAL
∧

SATARA
∧

TAMBOTI
∧

MAROELA
∧

ORPEN
∧

TALAMATI
∧

SKUKUZA
∧

LOWER SABIE
∧

PRETORIUSKOP
∧

BIYAMITI
∧

BERG-EN-DAL
∧

CROCODILE BRIDGE
∧

MALELANE
∧

Geology

	Basalt
	Dolerite/Gabbro
	Granite
	Karoo Shale/Sandstone
	Rhyolite
	Sand deposits
	Soutpansberg Sandstone/ Quartzite

0 20 40 60
Km

Landscape

Landscape	No.
Lowveld Sour Bushveld of Pretoriuskop	1
Malelane Mountain Bushveld	2
Weeping Bushwillow/Large-fruited Bushwillow Woodland	3
Thickets of the Sabie and Crocodile Rivers	4
Mixed Bushwillow/Silver Clusterleaf Woodland	5
Bushwillow/Mopane Woodland of the Timbavati-area	6
Olifants River Rugged Veld	7
Phalaborwa Sandveld	8
Mopane Savanna on Basic Soils	9
Letaba River Rugged Veld	10
Tsendze Sandveld	11
Mopane/Knob Thorn Savanna	12
Delagoa Thorn Thickets on Karoo Sediments	13
Kumana Sandveld	14
Mopane Forest	15
Punda Maria Sandveld on Cave Sandstone	16
Marula/Knob Thorn Savanna	17
Dwarf Knob Thorn Savanna	18
Thornveld on Gabbro	19
Bangu Rugged Veld	20
Bushwillow/Thorn Tree Rugged Veld	21
Bushwillow/Mopane Rugged Veld	22
Mopane Shrubveld on Basalt	23
Mopane Shrubveld on Gabbro	24
Baobab/Mopane Rugged Veld	25
Mopane Shrubveld on Calcrete	26
Mixed Bushwillow/Mopane Woodland	27
Limpopo/Levubu Floodplains	28
Lebombo South	29
Pumbe Sandveld	30
Lebombo North	31
Nwambiya Sandveld	32
Round-leaved Bloodwood/Weeping Bushwillow Woodland	33
Punda Maria Sandveld on Soutpansberg Sandstone	34
Narrow-leaved Mustardtree Floodplains	35

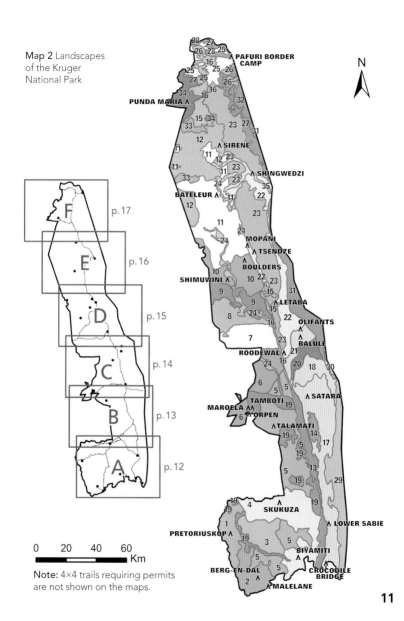

Map 2 Landscapes of the Kruger National Park

N

PAFURI BORDER CAMP

28 27
26 28 25
16
25 25 26
27 25 26

PUNDA MARIA ∧

34
16 16
33 15 34
12
11 ∧ SIRENE
11
11 12
11 23
33 23 ∧ SHINGWEDZI
24 23
BATELEUR ∧ 11
12

11

24
MOPANI ∧
∧ TSENDZE
∧ BOULDERS
10
SHIMUWINI ∧ 10 22 23
9 15
9 ∧ LETABA
8 15
24 22 OLIFANTS
16 ∧
7 23 BALULE
ROODEWAL ∧ 21
16
24 20 18 30

6
5 5
TAMBOTI ∧ 19 ∧ SATARA
MAROELA ∧∧
6 ∧ ORPEN
∧ TALAMATI
19 14
5 17
19
5 13
5 29
19

19 ∧ SKUKUZA 19
19 4 ∧ LOWER SABIE
PRETORIUSKOP ∧
19 3 5
5 BIYAMITI
∧
5 ∧ CROCODILE
BERG-EN-DAL 2 ∧ BRIDGE
∧ MALELANE

23 27 31

32

35
22

31

F p. 17
E p. 16
D p. 15
C p. 14
B p. 13
A p. 12

0   20   40   60
▬▬▬▬▬▬ Km

Note: 4×4 trails requiring permits are not shown on the maps.

11

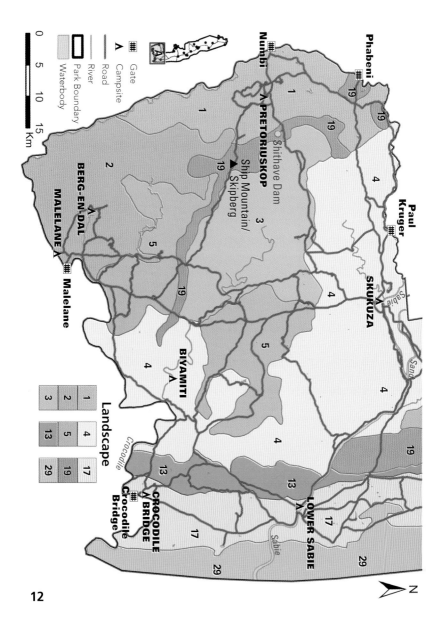

12

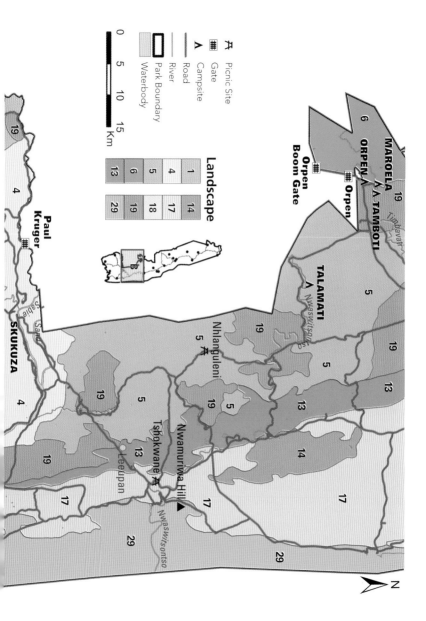

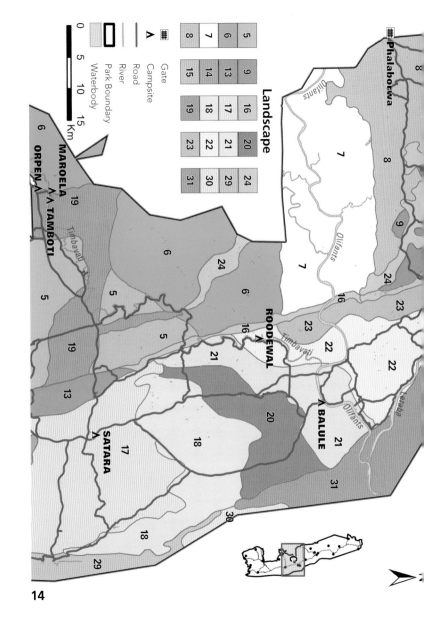

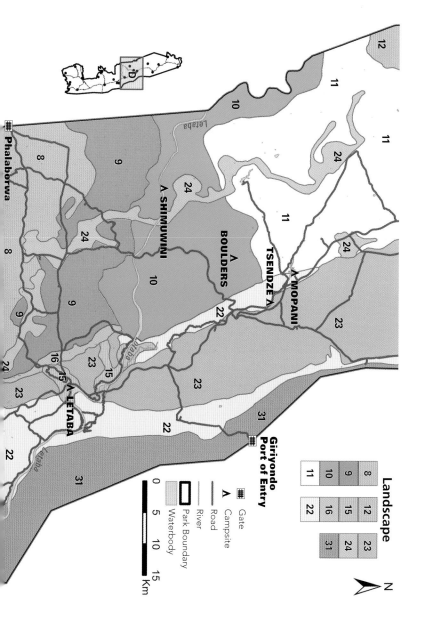

Landscape

8	12	23
9	15	24
10	16	31
11	22	

Phalaborwa

∧ SHIMUWINI

∧ BOULDERS

TSENDZE ∧
∧ MOPANI

∧ LETABA

Letaba

Giriyondo
Port of Entry

N

Legend

⌗ Gate
∧ Campsite
— Road
— River
▭ Park Boundary
▨ Waterbody

0 5 10 15
Km

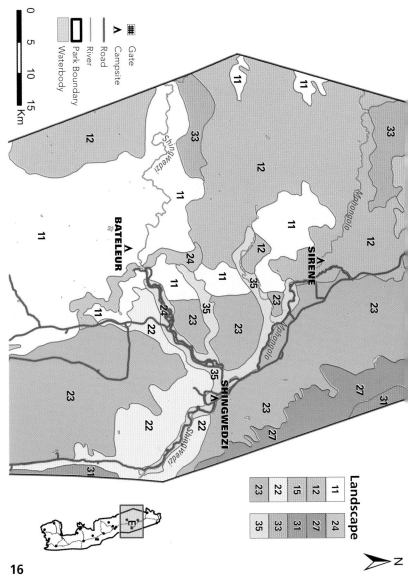

Landscape

11	12	15	22	23

24	27	31	33	35

Gate
Campsite
Road
River
Park Boundary
Waterbody

0 5 10 15
Km

N

16

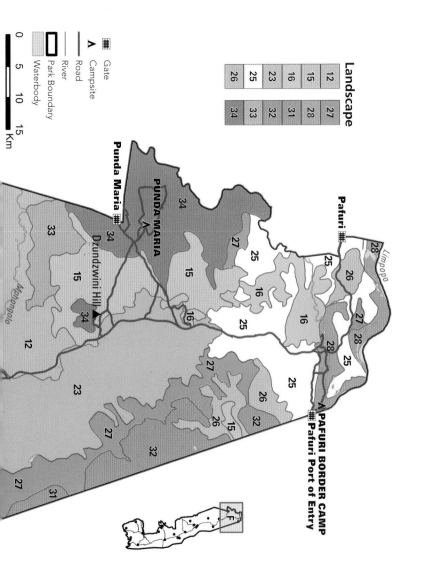

Landscape

12	27
15	28
16	31
23	32
25	33
26	34

Legend

⊞	Gate
▲	Campsite
—	Road
—	River
▢	Park Boundary
	Waterbody

0 5 10 15 Km

N

Punda Maria

PUNDA MARIA

Punda Maria ⊞

Dzundzwini Hill ▲

Pafuri ⊞

Limpopo

Mphongolo

PAFURI BORDER CAMP
▲ **Pafuri Port of Entry**

34
34
33
15
34
12
23
15
16
16
25
16
25
27
26
26
25
27
32
27
31
27
25
28
27
28
25
26
25
28
15
32

Checklist: landscapes and commonly found trees *

1 Lowveld Sour Bushveld of Pretoriuskop

red bushwillow	**p. 49**
weeping bushwillow	**p. 51**
large-fruited bushwillow	**p. 53**
sicklebush	**p. 59**
African-wattle	**p. 71**
marula	p. 75
green monkey-orange	p. 83
sycamore fig	p. 113
large-leaved false-thorn	p. 149
tasselberry	p. 151
mobolaplum	p. 157
camel's foot	p. 159
kiaat	p. 161
black monkey-orange	**p. 163**
silver clusterleaf	**p. 165**
paperbark thorn	p. 167
velvet bushwillow	**p. 173**
live-long	p. 189

2 Malelane Mountain Bushveld

red bushwillow	**p. 49**
weeping bushwillow	**p. 51**
large-fruited bushwillow	**p. 53**
sicklebush	p. 59
knob thorn	**p. 79**
purple-podded clusterleaf	p. 85
umbrella thorn	p. 93
silver clusterleaf	**p. 165**
broad-leaved coraltree	p. 177
common coraltree	p. 179
boekenhout	p. 183

3 Weeping Bushwillow/Large-fruited Bushwillow Woodland

red bushwillow	**p. 49**
weeping bushwillow	**p. 51**
large-fruited bushwillow	**p. 53**
zebrawood	p. 57
sicklebush	p. 59
jacketplum	p. 69
African-wattle	p. 71
round-leaved bloodwood	**p. 73**
marula	p. 75
knob thorn	p. 79
flaky-barked thorn	p. 87
jackalberry	p. 105
weeping boerbean	p. 129
black monkey-orange	p. 163
silver clusterleaf	**p. 165**
velvet bushwillow	p. 173

4 Thickets of the Sabie and Crocodile Rivers

greenthorn	p. 39
red bushwillow	**p. 49**
sicklebush	**p. 59**
knob thorn	**p. 79**
purple-podded clusterleaf	p. 85
magic guarri	**p. 109**
tamboti	p. 131
horned thorn	**p. 137**

5 Mixed Bushwillow/Silver Clusterleaf Woodland

red bushwillow	**p. 49**
large-fruited bushwillow	**p. 53**
zebrawood	p. 57
sicklebush	p. 59
false-marula	p. 65
African-wattle	p. 71
round-leaved bloodwood	p. 73
marula	p. 75
black monkey thorn	p. 77
knob thorn	**p. 79**
flaky-barked thorn	**p. 87**

* **Bolder** tree names = more abundant or conspicuous trees

6 Bushwillow/Mopane Woodland of the Timbavati-area

7 Olifants River Rugged Veld

8 Phalaborwa Sandveld

PLAINS

KOPPIES

Large-leaved rock fig.

Sunrise over open bushveld in the central part of Kruger.

18 Dwarf Knob Thorn Savanna

19 Thornveld on Gabbro

20 Bangu Rugged Veld

21 Bushwillow/Thorn Tree Rugged Veld

PLAINS

KOPPIES

22 Bushwillow/Mopane Rugged Veld

PLAINS

KOPPIES

23 Mopane Shrubveld on Basalt

24 Mopane Shrubveld on Gabbro

25 Baobab/Mopane Rugged Veld

26 Mopane Shrubveld on Calcrete

Grey Go-away-bird pauses while feeding on marula fruit.

27 Mixed Bushwillow/Mopane Woodland

30 Pumbe Sandveld

Only a small extension of this landscape occurs in the Park, in the vicinity of Pumbe, northeast of Satara. The terrain contains many trees that are rare elsewhere in the Park, so they have not been described in this book.

31 Lebombo North

Baobab in Kruger.

32 Nwambiya Sandveld

Contains a great diversity of woody plants, many of which are uncommon in the rest of the Park. Most of the species more or less confined to this landscape are not included in this book, and only some of the more common ones are listed below. The tree diversity of this landscape is not only unique in the Park, but also in South Africa.

33 Round-leaved Bloodwood/ Weeping Bushwillow Woodland

34 Punda Maria Sandveld on Soutpansberg Sandstone

Contains a great diversity of woody plants, many of which are uncommon in the rest of the Park. Most of the species more or less confined to this landscape are not included in this book and only some of the more common ones are listed below.

35 Narrow-leaved Mustardtree Floodplains

Identifying trees from a distance

It can be challenging to identify trees accurately from a distance, assisted only by photographs and some descriptive text. However, outside of the rest camps and in most parts of the Park, this is the only option available for visitors.

When making a tree ID, the overall shape is a good place to start, especially for more distinctive trees such as baobabs and palms. Shape is less reliable in less distinctive trees, so adopt a flexible view that allows for variation. Most individuals of a particular species may look rather different from the subject in a photograph, and also from each other – perhaps they will be smaller than the often-larger and particularly photogenic specimen picked out by a photographer, or they may have more stems.

More reliable identifiers are the colour and texture of a tree's foliage. These features are difficult to describe in words and photographs are helpful.

Bark features are also helpful as they are always available, but are most reliable in older trees, as there can be significant variance in younger trees – bark is almost always smooth in relatively young stems.

Red bushwillow, one of the most abundant trees in Kruger.

Flowers (especially when profuse and showy) and fruits are ideal to confirm identification, all the better if aided by binoculars, but remember that flowering and fruiting times are restricted to certain times of the year.

Many trees are deciduous, making them tricky to identify during the dormant season.

For a more detailed explanation on how the species accounts are presented, see pages 28–29.

How to use this book

To use this book effectively, two approaches to identify a tree are suggested: one general, the other more targeted.

The general page-through approach

Simply page through the photographs in this book and look for features that match the tree you wish to identify. A good starting point is to browse through the images in the group that best describes the habitat of the tree. For example, if the tree is on a riverbank, then the most appropriate habitat would be **rivers and floodplains** (pages 96–145). If silver clusterleaf is present and the soils look sandy, start with the trees of **deep sandy soils** (pages 146–167), and if the tree is on a rocky outcrop, begin with the trees of **koppies and rocky ridges** (pages 168–191). If you can't make a match in any of those groups, then look through the **generalists** (pages 32–95) to find your tree.

The 'landscapes' approach

Refer to Map 2 (pages 10–11) and select the enlarged map for the area through which you are travelling (pages 12–17). Each of the 35 landscapes in the Park has a name and corresponding number and colour on the maps. Use the key to note which landscape/s your journey will take you through. Next, locate the specific landscapes in the checklist (pages 18–25). For each landscape there is a list of common trees that occur there, each tree followed by the page number. (Particularly abundant or conspicuous trees appear in bold type.) Only trees included in this book are listed.

Look for a match among the trees given for a particular landscape. In some instances, and where appropriate, trees have been listed separately for plains and valleys, and rocky ridges and koppies.

Mopane worm feeding on mopane leaves.

Guide to the species accounts

The tree species in this book are organised into four groups – given below – according to each tree's habitat. This is by no means an infallible subdivision, but it is the simplest approach when there is no direct access to study leaves, flowers and fruit closely.

Generalists (pages 32–95) These trees may occur on various substrates and are often widespread in the Park.

Rivers and floodplains (pages 96–145) These trees grow on the banks of streams and rivers; those on associated floodplains often show a preference for brackish soils.

Deep sandy soils (pages 146–167) A few tree species with a preference for sandy soils are relatively widespread in the Park. Silver clusterleaf (see page 165) is a good indicator tree for sandy soil. However, many diverse restricted-range species are more or less confined to the Nwambiya Sandveld in the far northeastern corner of the Park and in the vicinity of Punda Maria. (Most of these rare species have not been included.)

Koppies and rocky ridges (pages 168–191) These trees preferentially grow among large rocks, not necessarily throughout the Park. Some are confined to the Lebombo range, others to the mountainous areas in the far south and far north. Because tourist roads often avoid very rocky areas, this book covers a relatively small number of tree species in this habitat.

○ **Group name**

○ **Common and scientific name**
English names are those most widely used in South Africa. Species are presented alphabetically in each group, according to their scientific name. Recent older scientific names are listed in the **Index** (page 199).

Fevertree
Vachellia xanthophloea

…edium-sized deciduous thorntree with a relatively long and …e main stem. The crown is spreading, sparse and usually …nded. Bark is exceptionally smooth, yellowish green and …vdery, sporadically peeling off in minute paper-thin flakes, or …ally as larger dark brown or black scales. Spines are in pairs, …aight and white. Leaves are borne in tufts and are twice-…nate. This species only grows in the eastern half of the Park …salt), in spruits and depressions, and next to rivers – it needs …ist conditions. There is an impressive stand of trees at Pafuri.

…ne wood is pale brown, without heartwood, and fairly hard and …eavy. It suffers severe damage by exceptionally large woodborers. …mber is suitable for furniture, carving and poles. Root and bark …re used in traditional medicine. Pods, leaves, branches and gum …re consumed by various wild animals; elephant may do extensive …amage. The trees were once mistakenly thought to be the cause …f malaria (hence the common name), because the malaria-carrying …nosquito and the tree prefer the same habitat.

○ **Description** focuses on features readily observed from a distance (or with binoculars). The opening sentence gives the typical height of the species:
  small up to 5 m
  medium 5–15 m
  large 15–30 m
  very large over 30 m

1 Flowers (spring) in bright yellow balls. **2** Pods (late summer) flat, straight …nd do not split open. **3** Bark unmistakable; smooth, yellowish green.

143

○ **Captions** include flowering and fruiting seasons, determined as follows:
  spring August–November
  summer November–March
  autumn March–May
  winter May–August

Technical terms have been kept to a minimum, but if you are unsure of a meaning, consult the **Glossary** at the back of the book (pages 192–195). Additional publications that may be consulted for further reading about trees in the Park are supplied in the **Bibliography** (page 196).

A large-leaved rock fig and klipspringer antelope, both associated with rocky habitats.

THE
TREES

Baobab

Adansonia digitata

A large deciduous tree with an unusually thick main trunk and a sparse roundish crown. The grey-brown to red-brown bark is smooth, with years of damage and growth rippling in folds and dents. This is one of the few trees that can form new bark over scarred areas. Mature leaves are alternate and palmately compound. Occurs from a few kilometres north of Tshokwane up to the Limpopo River. Very rare in the south.

The wood is soft, very light and spongy, and is used in paper production. The bark fibres are used to make rope and woven items. Tubers (at the root tips) are dried and ground for porridge. The fruit pulp makes a refreshing drink and is also used in traditional medicine. Leaves and oil-rich seed are eaten by humans. Primates eat the fruits, and elephant feed on leaves and stems. Cavities in the stems are favoured nesting sites for Böhm's Spinetail birds.

1

2

3

1 Flowers (spring–summer) unpleasantly scented, pendulous; mostly pollinated by bats. 2 Fruit (autumn) ± 120 mm long, with woody shell, densely covered with yellowish grey hair. 3 Mature baobab in leaf. Leafless branches (main photograph) resemble an upended root-system, hence the popular name – upside-down tree.

Bushveld false-thorn
Albizia harveyi

A small to medium-sized deciduous tree, or shrub, with a bare main stem, low-hanging branches and a dense, roundish, spreading crown. The bark is dark grey with prominent vertical ridges. Leaves are alternate and twice-pinnate. Occurs throughout the Park with larger specimens in alluvial soils on floodplains at Pafuri. Abundant in low-lying brackish areas.

The wood is fairly heavy, pale brown and without heartwood, with a fine texture that produces a sheer finish. It is, however, apparently rarely used. Browsers feed on the leaves.

1 Flowers (late spring) are creamy white, in fluffy heads. **2** Pods (late summer) are flat, thin-valved and swollen above each seed.

Many-stemmed false-thorn
Albizia petersiana subsp. *evansii*

A medium-sized, multi-stemmed deciduous tree with a V-shaped framework. The bark is grey with a yellow tinge and peels off in thin, flat irregular strips. Leaves are alternate, twice-pinnate. Abundant along the Karoo sediments, running north–south from Pafuri to Crocodile Bridge, but mainly in the area south of Satara and Orpen.

The wood is fairly hard and heavy, consisting of pale brown sapwood and a yellow to dark brown central area that produces a smooth wood finish. The bark and roots are used medicinally. Leaves are eaten by browsers, and young pods by giraffe.

1 Flowers (early summer) in loose heads, usually whitish with a central red 'stalk'. **2** Pods (late summer–autumn) are flat, brown to reddish purple.

Greenthorn
Balanites maughamii subsp. *maughamii*

A medium-sized to large deciduous to semi-deciduous tree with a distinctive long and straight main trunk with deep folds. The crown is fairly sparse, spreading and roundish (but slender in young trees). The bark is dark grey and rough, deeply fluted, and branches are armed with sturdy spines. Leaves are alternate and compound with two stalked leaflets. Occurs throughout the Park on sand and granitic soils, but is rare. Biggest specimens at Skukuza and along the Sabie River.

The wood is predominantly yellow and without heartwood. It is heavy and durable, useful for carving household items. The bark and roots are used medicinally and as a fish poison to stupefy fish, making them easy to catch. Leaves are eaten by elephant and giraffe, and the fruit by baboons and impala, among other animals. Seeds produce large quantities of edible oil that also burns well.

1 Flowers (spring) in clusters, tiny and inconspicuous, greenish yellow. **2** Fruit (autumn–winter) oval, ± 35 × 25 mm, thinly fleshy, hairy, yellow to light brown. **3** Trunks of older specimens have deep lengthwise folds.

Tree-wisteria

Bolusanthus speciosus

A small to medium-sized deciduous tree or shrub, usually multi-stemmed. It has a narrow crown with drooping foliage. Leaves are alternate, odd-pinnate and greyish green. The tree grows throughout the Park on a variety of soil types, with considerable numbers only on doleritic soils, such as those at Skipberg (Ship Mountain), west of Leeupan (Lion Pan), and at Shitlhave Dam.

The wood is fairly light, the sapwood off-white, and the heartwood brown with lighter blotches. It makes excellent timber for furniture, but the small size of available wood limits this use. Damaged bark exudes a red gum that contains a dye. Leaves are eaten by kudu and elephant, the latter often pushing the trees over to feed on them.

1 Flowers (spring) in loose, hanging clusters, pale blue to violet. **2** Pods (summer) flat and inconspicuous; do not split open. **3** Bark dark grey-brown with a rough texture and lengthwise grooves.

Shepherd's tree
Boscia albitrunca

A small to medium-sized semi-deciduous tree with a long main stem. The crown is twiggy, fairly dense and greyish green. The bark is smooth and light coloured to rough and greyish, breaking up in places, but not peeling off. Leaves are alternate or in tufts, simple. Occurs throughout the Park – abundant in the far north, especially around Pafuri, rarer in other parts, and in the south found only in rocky places.

The wood is without heartwood, off-white to pale yellow-brown. It is fairly heavy and used for manufacturing household articles. One of the most valuable fodder trees for game and domestic stock. Roots are used in traditional medicine, to make a porridge, as a substitute for coffee, and to brew beer. Fruits are edible but not tasty.

1 Flowers (spring) in axillary clusters, small and yellowish green. **2** Berries (summer) globose, ± 10 mm in diameter, hairless and yellowish, often with pinkish flush. Popular with birds.

Sjambokpod
Cassia abbreviata subsp. *beareana*

A small to medium-sized deciduous tree with a short, straight main stem. The crown is spreading and symmetrical, round to umbrella-shaped. The bark is rough, dark brown to black, with broad ridges running lengthwise. Leaves are alternate, even-pinnate. It occurs throughout the Park but is not abundant, although it can be seen south of Satara, along the Timbavati River and north of Balule.

The wood is heavy and hard and somewhat coarse in texture. Sapwood is light brown and heartwood dark brown with lighter blotches. The bark and roots are used medicinally. It is seldom eaten by game. Seeds and the greenish pulp inside the pods are eagerly consumed by birds, including Green Wood Hoopoe, Grey and Yellow-billed hornbills and Crested Barbet.

1 Flowers (spring) usually abundant before or with the new leaves, yellow.
2 Pods (winter–spring) pendulous, up to 900 mm long, cylindrical, splitting open while on the tree.

Mopane
Colophospermum mopane

A medium-sized deciduous tree or shrub. The crown is upright, poorly spreading and rarely rounded. The bark is grey to almost white (on the side that receives the most sun), otherwise dark grey and deeply grooved lengthwise. Leaves are alternate and compound. Its shrubby growth form is ascribed mainly to soil condition and also veld fires. The most abundant tree in the Park other than the red bushwillow, covering almost the entire area north of the Olifants River. Also occurs west of the Timbavati River just about down to Orpen Rest Camp. On the Lebombo range it extends south of the Olifants River.

The wood is attractive, with sapwood off-white to light brown, and heartwood mainly dark brown and blotched. The timber is used for furniture, curios and firewood. The bark yields a strong fibre. Leaves are browsed by domestic stock, especially during dry spells, and by game. Twigs and leaves are an important part of the diet of the elephant. The leaves are eaten by the larvae of an emperor moth, commonly known as mopane worms, which are known to denude large stands of leaves.

1 Flowers (summer) inconspicuous, greenish, with long-protruding stamens.
2 Fruit (autumn) flattened, weakly kidney-shaped, does not split open.
3 Leaves have two leaflets forming a characteristic butterfly shape. They smell strongly of turpentine when crushed.

Red bushwillow

Combretum apiculatum subsp. *apiculatum*

A small to medium-sized, often multi-stemmed deciduous tree, with leaves that turn brownish red in autumn. The main stem is relatively short and slightly crooked. The crown is sparse and spreading. The bark is grey to greyish black, cracking into small, flat, irregular blocks. Leaves are opposite, simple. Apart from mopane, this is probably the most abundant tree in the Park. Occurs on granitic and rhyolitic soils as well as in rocky areas on basalt plains adjacent to the Lebombo range. The biggest specimens are found south of the Olifants River.

The wood is very hard and heavy, and is used for fencing posts and fuel – coals can last up to 12 hours. Heartwood is dark brown to black, sapwood pale to yellow-brown. Leaves are used medicinally. Seeds are eaten by the Brown-headed Parrot, but are said to be poisonous to humans, causing prolonged hiccupping. This is a good fodder plant for domestic stock as well as game. Also a larval food plant for the Striped Policeman butterfly.

1 Flowers (spring) in short axillary spikes, creamy yellow. Leaf tips are usually conspicuously twisted. **2** Fruit (summer–autumn) four-winged, up to 25 × 30 mm, with a sticky varnish-like cover when young.

Weeping bushwillow

Combretum collinum subsp. *suluense*

A small to medium-sized deciduous tree, with leaves turning yellow in autumn. Stems are mostly short, crooked and screened by shoots sprouting from the base. The crown is quite dense, upright and slightly spreading, with the lowest branches and tips of branchlets drooping. The bark is fairly rough, sporadically peeling off in irregular sections and usually without ridges running lengthwise. Leaves are opposite, simple. Occurs in granitic soils throughout the western half of the Park, as well as in rhyolitic soils on the Lebombo Mountains; only abundant in the Pretoriuskop, Malelane and Punda Maria areas.

The wood is hard and fairly heavy, undifferentiated, yellow-brown to brown. Leaves are browsed by game.

1 Flowers (spring) in axillary spikes, creamy yellow. **2** Fruit (summer–autumn) four-winged, up to 45 × 50 mm, dark reddish brown when young, ripening to dark brown, densely covered in fine hairs.

Large-fruited bushwillow
Combretum zeyheri

A small to medium-sized deciduous tree, with leaves turning pale yellow in autumn. The main stem is relatively short and mostly slender, and the tree is often multi-stemmed. The crown is slightly spreading and rather sparse; new shoots are densely hairy. The bark is fairly smooth, but there are rough patches where it peels off in small, irregular blocks. Leaves are opposite, simple. Found everywhere and in abundance in the Park, with the exception of the Lebombo plains (basalt) and brackish flats, thus occurring on granite, sand and rhyolite. Especially prominent in the Pretoriuskop, Skukuza and Malelane areas.

Freshly cut wood is bright yellow, drying to pale yellow. The timber is medium-heavy, fairly hard and tough, but not particularly durable. Leaves are poorly browsed by game. Gum is edible and considered a delicacy by humans. The bark and leaves are used medicinally. The fibrous roots are used for weaving items such as baskets. The fruit is a larval food source for the Apricot Playboy butterfly, with the larvae in turn often skilfully removed from the fruit and consumed by the Southern Black Tit.

1 Flowers (spring) appear together with new leaves, in relatively long axillary spikes, greenish yellow. **2** Fruit (late summer–autumn) is four-winged, large (up to 80 × 80 mm), yellowish green, ripening to pale brown. **3** Bark whitish to greyish brown, relatively smooth.

Tall common corkwood

Commiphora glandulosa

A small deciduous tree with a fairly short, rather thick and straight main stem, often screened by lateral branchlets. The crown is relatively dense and roughly round, twiggy with drooping branchlets, with some twigs ending in grey-brown thorns. The bark usually peels off in small, paper-thin, yellow flakes or large, curled sections, sometimes as small, dark grey blocks. Leaves are alternate or in tufts, usually simple, rarely compound with three leaflets, with cloudy latex. Enjoys a wide north–south distribution on basalt and rhyolite (Lebombo) on the eastern side of the Park. Abundant in the Balule and Pafuri areas.

The wood is very soft and light, coarsely grained and dirty white, without heartwood. Commonly used for household utensils. Leaves are browsed by game; fruit eaten by birds. Often planted as a living fence.

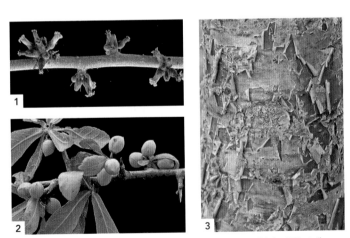

1 Flowers (spring) are small and inconspicuous, pink or reddish. **2** Fruit (late summer–autumn) is fleshy and reddish when ripe, containing a blackish seed partly covered by a bright red, fleshy appendage (aril). **3** Bark greenish, flaking in small, yellowish papery pieces.

Zebrawood

Dalbergia melanoxylon

A multi-stemmed shrub or small, deciduous, thorny tree. The stems are grooved and dented, usually low branching, and sometimes screened by lateral branchlets. The crown is sparse, rather poorly spreading and twiggy. The bark is grey and fairly smooth, peeling off in flat, irregular strips. Leaves are alternate, odd-pinnate. Found throughout the Park, but especially common in the southern area at Skukuza and Pretoriuskop; however, very dense stands of shrubs are found only on basalt and dolerite.

The sapwood is narrow and a dirty to bright yellow, while the heartwood is pitch-black, sometimes with dark brown striations, hence the common name. The timber is very hard, finely textured, heavy and exceptionally durable, making it suitable for ornamental work. Elephant relish the roots. Leaves are consumed by various browsers.

1 Flowers (spring–summer) in small clusters towards branch tips, pea-like, white. **2** Pods (autumn) flat, thin, papery and hairless; do not split open.

Sicklebush
Dichrostachys cinerea

A multi-stemmed shrub or small deciduous tree with an untidy, spreading crown, flat-topped or rounded with lax branches. The bark is grey-brown and shallowly grooved lengthwise. Spines are single, same colour as the branchlets. Leaves are alternate or in tufts, twice-pinnate (feathery), with leaflets less than 2 mm wide (subsp. *africana* – small-leaved sicklebush) or more than 2 mm wide (subsp. *nyassana* – large-leaved sicklebush). Occurs throughout the Park. Subsp. *africana* is abundant on the brackish soils south of the Sabie River as well as on parts of the Lebombo flats (basalt). Subsp. *nyassana* is common in the Pretoriuskop area, more or less confined to the granitic and sandy soils in the western half of the Park.

This wood is exceptionally hard, heavy and durable. Sapwood is light brown to yellow-brown, heartwood dark brown. Makes excellent firewood. Cords and ropes are made from bark fibres. Leaves, bark and roots are used in traditional medicine. The highly nutritious pods are eaten by game and livestock.

1 Flowers (spring–summer) in hanging spikes; the pinky-mauve part is sterile, yellow flowers are fertile. **2** Pods (summer–autumn) in dense clusters, curly and twisted.

Wildpear

Dombeya rotundifolia var. *rotundifolia*

A small to medium-sized deciduous tree with a short, crooked main stem, often with a few lateral twigs. The crown is sparse to fairly dense, round but mostly formless. The bark is dark grey, breaking up into irregular blocks. Leaves are alternate, simple, with 3–6 prominent veins from the base. Found on granitic and rhyolitic as well as sandy soils. It is especially abundant in the Pretoriuskop and Malelane areas, also on the Lebombo plains and near Punda Maria.

The wood is heavy, tough and undifferentiated, yellow-brown to brown. It is used for furniture, ornaments and implement handles, and was considered one of the best timbers for wagon-building (hubs, felloes, spokes). The bark, roots and leaves are used in traditional medicine. The bark fibre is used to make ropes. It is not much utilised by game.

1 Flowers (late winter–early spring) are produced in profusion before the new leaves, white fading to brown. **2** Fruit (summer) a small capsule, surrounded by persistent dried petals.

Giant raisin

Grewia hexamita

A small deciduous tree with a short, somewhat crooked main stem fluted with lengthwise folds. The crown is sparse, and formless or roundish. The bark is dark grey and rough, breaking up into vertical ridges. Leaves are alternate, simple and glossy, with the base often strongly asymmetrical. Grows throughout the Park on all soil types, but never in dense stands.

The wood is heavy, not very hard, and the yellow-brown sapwood contrasts in colour with the brown heartwood. Used for household utensils. Fruits are eaten by humans, birds and other animals, but are not particularly tasty. Leaves are eaten by a variety of browsers such as elephant, kudu, giraffe and impala.

1 Flowers (spring) borne in axillary clusters, yellow. **2** Fruit (summer) thinly fleshy, globose or deeply two-lobed, up to 20 mm in diameter, yellow.

63

False-marula

Lannea schweinfurthii var. *stuhlmannii*

A small to medium-sized deciduous tree with a relatively short and straight main stem. The crown is mostly round but often asymmetrical, and branch tips are often drooping. The bark is smooth, brown-grey, and peels off sporadically in oval strips or flakes, leaving paler blotches. Leaves are alternate and odd-pinnate, turning yellow or white on some branches in late summer. Occurs throughout the Park. Abundant in and around Skukuza, as well as between Tshokwane and Satara.

The wood is fairly light, off-white and undifferentiated, medium-hard. It is easy to work with but does not finish smoothly. Damaged by insects when dry. The bark, leaves and roots are used medicinally. Fruits taste good and are eaten by humans (not the skins). They are also popular with birds and other fruit-eating animals. Leaves are widely consumed by browsing game. The peculiar fur-like velvety hairs on the root bark make this tree highly valued for its alleged supernatural powers.

1 Flowers (late spring–summer) in drooping spikes, small, creamy white.
2 Fruit (summer) is fleshy, reddish to dark brown when ripe. **3** Leaves fresh pale green on both sides; seen here with flower buds.

Weeping resintree

Ozoroa engleri

A small semi-deciduous tree or shrub, with a short main stem that is usually bent. The crown is spreading and roundish, with branchlets and greyish green foliage both drooping. The bark is dark grey-brown to nearly black and rough, cracking into small irregular blocks. Leaves are opposite or in whorls of three, simple, with whitish latex. Widespread in the Park, but nowhere in great abundance. Most occur on the basalt plains south of the Olifants River as well as on the Lebombo range.

The wood is fairly light and hard, undifferentiated, and dark brown with a reddish tinge. It is easy to work with but apparently not used much. Extracts of the bark, leaves and roots are used in traditional medicine. Leaves are eaten by browsers.

1 Flowers (late spring–summer) in often drooping terminal clusters, small, white. **2** Fruit (summer–autumn) thinly fleshy, kidney-shaped, ripening to black and wrinkled.

Jacketplum

Pappea capensis

A small deciduous to evergreen tree, often multi-stemmed, with a short and somewhat crooked main stem. Specimens on brackish flats along rivers have a dense, spreading and round crown; on koppies and mountains the species has a slender, sparse crown. The bark is fairly smooth, grey or nearly white, and peels off sporadically. Leaves are alternate or in tufts, simple. Occurs throughout the Park; in the south on brackish flats as well as mountains and koppies, but in the north only on stony areas.

The wood is tough, fairly heavy, undifferentiated, and pale brown with a reddish tinge. It is rarely used except for firewood. Roots, bark and leaves are used in traditional medicine. Twigs and leaves are edible, making it an excellent fodder plant for game and domestic stock. The seeds yield an edible though slightly purgative oil, which is also used medicinally. The fleshy covering around the seeds is edible, with a pleasant sweet-sour taste, and makes a delicious jam.

1 Flowers (summer–autumn) borne in drooping spikes, small, greenish yellow.
2 Fruit (spring–summer) a one- to three-lobed, furry, green capsule, splitting open to reveal a shiny black seed enclosed by a fleshy red or orange-red covering.

African-wattle

Peltophorum africanum

A small to medium-sized deciduous tree, with a low-branching main stem. The crown is widely spreading, fairly dense and sometimes roundish. The bark is rough, dark grey-brown and shallowly grooved lengthwise. Leaves are alternate and twice-pinnate, creating a feathery appearance. Occurs throughout the Park in all soil types, but bigger and more abundant in the Pretoriuskop and Lebombo areas.

The sapwood is off-white and narrow, the heartwood is dark brown and asymmetrical; used as general-purpose timber and firewood. The bark and roots are used medicinally. Leaves are browsed by game. Several butterflies of the genera *Charaxes* (emperors) and *Axiocerses* (scarlets) breed on the tree. Sap-sucking spittle bugs occasionally visit the branches and excrete large quantities of foamy liquid that drips from the tree, hence the other common name 'weeping-wattle'.

1 Flowers (late spring–summer) in erect clusters, yellow, conspicuous.
2 Pods (summer) are flat, thickened in the middle, winged.

Round-leaved bloodwood
Pterocarpus rotundifolius subsp. *rotundifolius*

Mostly a multi-stemmed deciduous shrub, but occasionally a small to medium-sized tree, with a widely spreading, relatively sparse crown. The bark is light grey to grey-brown, cracking lengthwise and peeling off in irregular flat strips. Leaves are alternate and odd-pinnate. Occurs everywhere in the Park except on the Lebombo flats, the Pafuri area (basalt) and the sandveld regions, particularly those around Pretoriuskop and Punda Maria, and the sandveld of Nwambiya.

The wood is fairly light, soft and yellow, without heartwood. It is an inferior-quality timber and smells unpleasant when freshly sawn, but nevertheless is used for manufacturing household articles. The species is consumed by browsers, especially elephant. Leaves are the larval food of the Bushveld Charaxes and Veined Paradise Skipper butterflies.

1 Flowers (late spring) in large branched inflorescences, deep yellow. **2** Pods (summer–autumn) flat, almost round in outline, and thickened over the usually single seed.

73

Marula

Sclerocarya birrea subsp. *caffra*

A medium-sized deciduous tree with a mostly straight and relatively long main stem. The crown is roundish, widely spreading and fairly dense. The bark is more or less smooth, peeling off sporadically in rather large, flat, roundish discs, exposing yellowish bark underneath. Leaves are alternate, odd-pinnate. Occurs throughout the Park, especially on basalt. Abundant on the Lebombo plains.

The wood is fairly light, off-white with a reddish tinge, and exceptionally tough. It is used for household items including traditional African mortars and pestles, drums and ornaments. Fruits are edible, tasty and nutritious, and popular for making beer and flavouring liqueur. Edible nuts are extracted from the hard seeds. Fruits and leaves are consumed by a large variety of wild animals. The bark is stripped by elephant. The tree is also widely used medicinally.

1 Flowers (spring) small, yellowish, tinged with pink; male and female flowers occur on different trees. **2** Fruit (summer) is fleshy, almost spherical, up to 40 mm in diameter, ripening to yellow after falling to the ground.

Black monkey thorn
Senegalia burkei

A medium-sized deciduous thorntree with a long, straight main stem, which is high-branching with a spreading, roundish crown. The bark breaks up into thick, grey, vertical ridges, with yellow in the grooves. Spines are in pairs, hooked, greyish black, sometimes borne on knobs. Leaves are alternate and twice-pinnate. Occurs mainly on granite, which is on the western side of the Park, especially south of the Olifants River, often in low-lying areas. Also found in other areas such as the Lebombo range.

The wood is yellow-brown, very hard, and heavy. It is used for the manufacture of furniture and household articles. Bark and leaves are used medicinally. Leaves are eaten by browsers, especially giraffe and elephant.

1 Flowers (spring) in elongated spikes, cream or white. **2** Pods (winter) flat, straight, reddish to purplish brown.

Knob thorn

Senegalia nigrescens

A medium-sized to large deciduous thorntree with a long, bare main stem. The crown is spreading and fairly dense. The bark is dark grey with deep vertical grooves. Spines are in pairs, hooked and black. Leaves are alternate and twice-pinnate, with large leaflets (10–30 mm in diameter). Found throughout the Park. Abundant on the basaltic soils in the eastern half of the Park between the Crocodile and Olifants rivers, as well as on doleritic soils. Also on low-lying granitic soils. Seldom on the sandy soils at Pretoriuskop.

The sapwood is dirty yellow; heartwood is dark brown, very hard, and heavy. The timber is used for furniture and makes good fence posts; also an excellent fuel. The species is a valuable fodder plant with leaves and pods consumed by a variety of browsers such as elephant and giraffe. Unripe seeds are eaten by Brown-headed Parrots.

1 Flowers (winter–spring) borne in elongated spikes, pale cream to pale yellow. **2** Pods (summer) are flat, dark greyish black when ripe. **3** Bark often has persistent spines on raised corky knobs on older stems and branches.

Delagoa thorn

Senegalia welwitschii subsp. *delagoensis*

A medium-sized deciduous thorntree with a straightish main stem, often screened by smaller branchlets. The crown is spreading, with dark green foliage creating a layered appearance. The bark is pale grey, and yellowish in the cracks between the lengthwise ridges. Spines are in pairs, short, hooked and black. Leaves are alternate or in tufts, twice-pinnate. Confined to the area south of the Olifants River, mainly on the contact between granite (west) and basalt (east). Isolated patches also occur elsewhere, such as along the Lower Sabie and Nhlanguleni roads.

The wood is heavy and very hard, with yellow-brown sapwood and black heartwood. It is difficult to saw and not insect-proof. The species is an important food plant for browsers, especially impala, elephant and giraffe, often leaving a distinct browse line showing the height of feeding.

1 Flowers (late spring–summer) borne in elongated spikes, yellowish white. **2** Pods (autumn–winter) straight, flat, deep wine-red to purple when immature, and ripening reddish brown to grey.

Green monkey-orange
Strychnos spinosa

A small to medium-sized deciduous tree with a relatively short, bare and usually crooked main stem. The crown is sparse and twiggy, upright to widely spreading. The bark is yellow-grey to grey, splitting into lengthwise ridges or flat, irregular sections. Spines are usually in opposite pairs, short, curved or straight, on branchlets. Leaves are opposite and simple. Distributed throughout the Park, especially in sandy and/or stony areas as well as on riverbanks. Rare on the basalt plains along the Lebombo range.

The wood is medium-heavy, pale brown and easy to work. Fruit pulp is edible and relished by humans and wildlife; it may be dried and stored for later use. The dry fruit shell is used as a container and as a sound box in traditional musical instruments. Many medicinal uses have been reported (contains strychnine-type alkaloids). Leaves are browsed by game.

1 Flowers (spring–summer) borne in compact heads, small, greenish white. **2** Fruit (spring–summer) is large, up to 120 mm in diameter, globose, yellowish brown when ripe.

Purple-podded clusterleaf

Terminalia prunioides

A multi-stemmed shrub or small, deciduous to semi-deciduous tree with mostly crooked and low-branching stems. The crown is fairly spreading, particularly twiggy, roundish and medium-dense. Bark is rough, subdivided lengthwise into ridges, pale to dark grey but brown in the grooves. Leaves are in clusters or alternate, and simple. Occurs throughout the Park on almost all soil types, but it seems to prefer soils with a high clay content, like the brackish flats, and stony areas. Abundant in the dense bush along the Sabie River.

The wood is heavy, hard, tough, undifferentiated, and brown. It is used for building huts and making implement handles. It is also an excellent firewood. The bark is used medicinally. Leaves and pods are consumed by browsing game and livestock.

1 Flowers (spring–summer) borne in slender axillary spikes, white to cream, often tinged with pink. **2** Fruit (summer–winter) is flat, surrounded by a wing, bright red to purple-red, drying to brown.

85

Flaky-barked thorn

Vachellia exuvialis

Either a multi-stemmed shrub or a small, single-stemmed, deciduous thorntree with a shiny orange-brown main stem. The crown is sparse and often V-shaped. Spines are in pairs, straight and white. The bark peels off in thin flakes to reveal a smooth, shiny coppery surface beneath. Leaves are alternate and twice-pinnate. Occurs mainly on granitic soils; very common in the Skukuza, Pretoriuskop and Malelane areas.

Despite the tree's abundance in the Park, relatively little is known about its uses and ecological significance. The flowers are a food source for a large range of insects. Leaves and pods are eaten by game and are particularly popular with giraffe (pods), impala and duiker; the spine length increases in response to browsing.

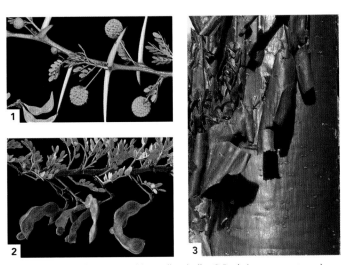

1 Flowers (spring) borne in golden-yellow balls. **2** Pods (summer–autumn) sickle-shaped, reddish brown when mature. **3** Bark peels off in large, thin, yellow to orange-brown flakes.

Red thorn
Vachellia gerrardii subsp. *gerrardii*

A small to medium-sized deciduous thorntree with a long, straight main stem branching high up, often screened by small branches. The crown is spreading, fairly sparse and somewhat flattened. The bark is black and deeply grooved lengthwise. Spines are in pairs, straight and white. Leaves are alternate and twice-pinnate. Widely distributed in the Park on almost all soil types, but more abundant in low-lying areas with poorly drained, brackish soils.

The wood is off-white with a brown tinge, fairly hard and medium-heavy. It is generally severely damaged by woodborers and apparently not used. The bark is used in traditional medicine and the inner bark provides a fibre used to plait ropes. Leaves and pods are eaten by browsers.

1 Flowers (spring–summer) in creamy white balls. **2** Pods (winter) curved, velvety-grey, splitting open while still on the tree.

Sweet thorn

Vachellia karroo

A small to medium-sized deciduous thorntree. The main stem is usually low branching, but in the Malelane Mountains it is long and clean. The crown is spreading and roundish, but slender in the Malelane Mountains. The bark is black or dark grey, and cracked lengthwise into narrow, irregular ridges. Spines are in pairs, straight and white, and may be absent on some branches. Leaves are alternate or in tufts, and twice-pinnate. Mainly confined to the Pretoriuskop and Malelane areas, but there are also a few specimens northwest of Punda Maria. The name *V. karroo* is used here in a broad sense; some of the trees identified as such in the Park may be *V. natalitia*.

The wood is off-white to pale brown, fairly hard and heavy. It is generally severely damaged by insects, but may be used for furniture, fence poles and firewood. Gum exuding from wounds on the stem is edible and consumed by humans and animals. The bark is used in traditional medicine. The inner bark is rich in fibre and used to manufacture baskets and ropes. Leaves and pods are eaten by game.

1 Flowers (summer) borne in bright yellow balls. **2** Pods (late summer–autumn) flat, curved and brown, splitting open while still on the tree.

Umbrella thorn

Vachellia tortilis subsp. *heteracantha*

A distinctive, medium-sized, deciduous thorntree with a fairly short, bare, sometimes crooked main stem. The crown is exceptionally widelyand usually umbrella-shaped. The bark is dark grey and deeply grooved lengthwise. Spines are in pairs and white. Leaves are in clusters and twice-pinnate. Occurs throughout most of the Park, but abundant only in certain areas. The largest specimens are near the rivers – such as the Luvuvhu, Tsendze and Timbavati – and larger spruits.

The sapwood is pale brown and the heartwood red-brown and very hard. It is not popular as timber but an important source of firewood. Gum exuded from wounds in the bark is edible. Pods and leaves are nutritious and browsed by stock and game. The bark is eaten by elephant and also used medicinally.

1 Flowers (spring–summer) in white balls. **2** Pods (autumn–winter) cylindrical, spirally twisted, and do not split open while on the tree. **3** Spines occur in various combinations of short and hooked, long and straight.

Buffalo-thorn

Ziziphus mucronata

A small to medium-sized deciduous tree, with leaves turning yellow in autumn. The main stem is rather short and crooked; the crown is sparse, spreading, usually with drooping branchlets. Foliage is typically glossy. Bark is pale grey, cracking into irregular, fibrous, elongated strips that peel off sporadically. Spines are in pairs, one hooked, the other straight; some forms are thornless (Pretoriuskop). Leaves are alternate and simple. Widespread in the Park on all soil types, occurring in larger numbers on brackish flats.

The wood has a narrow, pale yellow-brown outer layer and a large, pale brown to brown central core. It is fairly heavy, tough and elastic, and used for axe handles, household utensils and other general functions. The bark, leaves and roots are used for traditional medicine, and magical and religious purposes. Fruits are edible but not tasty, and are fermented for beer. Leaves, which grow fairly fast and are cold resistant, are browsed by game as well as domestic stock.

1 Flowers (spring–summer) borne in axillary clusters, small, yellowish green.
2 Fruit (summer–winter) globose, turning dark brown, shiny. **3** Spines in pairs, one hooked, the other straight.

95

Matumi

Breonadia salicina

A very large evergreen tree with an erect main stem. The crown may be sparse to dense, but is generally poorly spreading, with side branchlets arranged in groups. Bark is grey-brown with irregular ridges running vertically. Leaves are in whorls of four, simple, and glossy dark green above. Occurs along all the rivers and other permanent water sources throughout the Park. Seldom found near large, dry watercourses. Planted in some rest camps.

The wood is heavy and fairly hard, with an oily quality. It is pale to dark brown with paler blotches, finely grained and durable, making it good material for parquet flooring, boats and furniture. The bark is used medicinally. Leaves are browsed by game.

1 Flowers (late spring–summer) in compact balls, pale yellow with a pinkish tinge. **2** Fruit (summer) a cluster of very small capsules.

Russet bushwillow
Combretum hereroense

A shrub or small to medium-sized deciduous tree with short, crooked main stems. The crown is medium-dense, sometimes rounded, with greyish green foliage. Bark is pale grey to black, rough, subdivided lengthwise. It peels off in long, narrow strips which sometimes crack crosswise. Leaves are opposite, simple. Occurs throughout the Park, more often along rivers and streams, and in low-lying areas such as brackish flats. Also shows a slight preference for rocky situations.

The wood is fairly heavy, undifferentiated, yellow-brown to brown. It is very hard, tough and durable; used for kraal fences and fuel. The long, straight shoots that sprout upward from the branches make it a popular choice for walking- and fighting-sticks. Gum from wounds is eaten by bushbabies (galagos). Browsed by cattle and game such as kudu, steenbok, elephant and giraffe. Bark and roots are used medicinally. Mature fruit is used to brew a traditional and tasty tea that is consumed without apparent ill effects. (Consumption of seeds of some bushwillows is said to cause hiccups.)

1 Flowers (spring) in axillary spikes, greenish yellow. **2** Fruit (summer) four-winged, ± 20 × 20 mm, wings pale brown, central part dark reddish brown.

Leadwood
Combretum imberbe

A medium-sized to large deciduous tree with a long, thick main stem; stems in older specimens are conspicuously pale grey, nearly white. The crown is widely spreading and rather sparse, roundish to slightly umbrella-shaped, with greyish foliage. The bark is cracked into a mesh of closely packed rectangular blocks. Leaves are opposite, simple. Found throughout the Park, mostly in low-lying areas along rivers and streams, but on basalt (Lebombo flats) it usually occurs in association with knob thorn and marula.

The wood is exceptionally hard and heavy, very difficult to work. Sapwood narrow and yellowish, heartwood dark brown to black. Used for kraals, fences and traditional African mortars; also suitable for ornamental work as well as furniture. It makes excellent firewood. The gum is a traditional food. Leaves are consumed by browsers and used medicinally by humans. Some trees have been carbon dated at over a thousand years. Because of the extreme hardness of the wood, dead trees may remain standing for many decades. Traditionally the species is regarded by some cultures – notably the Herero in Namibia – as having mystical properties.

1 Flowers (spring) in smallish axillary spikes, whitish yellow. **2** Fruit (autumn) four-winged, ± 15 × 15 mm, pale yellowish green. **3** Bark pale grey to almost white; cracked into small rectangular blocks.

Feverberry
Croton megalobotrys

A shrub or small to medium-sized deciduous tree with a short and bent main stem. The crown is dense and round, with the lowest branches drooping. The bark is fairly smooth and grey-brown with a yellow tinge; the outer layer of bark divides into lengthwise strips. Leaves are alternate, simple, four- or five-veined from the base, with watery latex. Only occurs on alluvial soil near rivers and spruits. Abundant north of Satara; rare in the southern parts.

The wood is white to off-white, without heartwood; it is light, soft, and easy to work with. The bark is used for treatment of malaria, and as a fish poison. Seeds are used as a laxative. Plants are extensively consumed by elephant, especially at Letaba and Pafuri.

1 Flowers (spring) borne in sturdy spikes, yellowish green, inconspicuous.
2 Fruit (summer) is a woody capsule up to 40 mm in diameter, yellowish brown when ripe.

103

Jackalberry

Diospyros mespiliformis

A medium-sized to large deciduous tree, with leaves turning dark yellow in autumn. The main stem is long, bare and straight. The widely spreading crown is dense and more or less rounded. Bark is dark grey to black, and peels off in small, flat sections. Leaves are alternate and simple, often with a wavy margin. Found throughout the Park on all soil types, but markedly associated with low-lying areas along rivers and streams, where it also attains maximum dimensions. Older trees often grow on termite mounds.

The wood is fairly heavy and hard; pale red with a brownish tone. It is durable, suitable as a general-purpose timber. Bark and leaves are used medicinally. Ends of twigs have been traditionally used as toothbrushes. Fruit is edible and palatable for humans and animals, including jackal, hence the common name; also used to brew beer, or dried and stored for later use. Leaves are sporadically consumed by browsers.

1 Flowers (spring) axillary, creamy white and inconspicuous. **2** Fruit (ripening slowly, about one year after flowering) a berry with a bristle-like tip, ± 22 mm in diameter, glossy, yellow to purplish. **3** Leaves of new growth often reddish; note young fruit.

Bushveld-saffron

Elaeodendron transvaalense

A small to medium-sized, deciduous or semi-deciduous tree, with leaves shedding over a very short time in summer. The main stem is short and mostly crooked. The crown is sparse but spreading, round and very twiggy, with drooping branchlets. Bark is dark grey or black and breaks up into small blocks. Leaves are alternate or in tufts, simple. Common but sparsely distributed. It does not require specific habitat conditions, but favours low-lying brackish areas in the granitic western half of the Park.

The wood is heavy and hard, finely textured, brown with a reddish tinge. It is also insect resistant. It is widely used for making household articles. The bark and roots are extensively prescribed in traditional medicine. Fruits are edible but not very tasty, eaten by birds. Leaves are browsed by game and livestock.

1 Flowers (summer) in axillary clusters, small, greenish white. **2** Fruit (winter–spring) fleshy, globose to oval, up to 15 mm in diameter, cream or pale yellow.

Magic guarri
Euclea divinorum

A multi-stemmed evergreen shrub or small tree with stems almost white, grey or dark grey with rough, black protuberances. The crown is rather dense, twiggy and roundish. Bark on the very old stems is rough and broken into small sections. Leaves are more or less opposite, simple, with a strongly wavy margin. Occurs throughout the Park. Often found in nearly homogeneous stands on brackish flats.

The wood is medium-heavy, hard and tough, pale red to red-brown, finely grained. It is used for small items, including knobkerries. The tree is said to have supernatural powers (hence the common name) so it is not used as firewood. Root bark is a source of dye to colour palm leaves used in basketry. Fruits are edible, but rather unpalatable and purgative. They are eaten by birds and used to brew an alcoholic beverage. Twigs may be used as toothbrushes. Branches are used in fire-fighting. Leaves are very seldom browsed by game.

1 Flowers (spring) are unisexual (male and female on separate plants) and borne in axillary clusters, small, white to cream. **2** Berries (autumn) globose, dull red-brown, often with a thin layer of white waxy powder.

Anatree

Faidherbia albida

A medium-sized to large deciduous thorntree that sheds its leaves in summer. The main stem is long and bare, branching higher up. Young trees are slender, older ones have widely spreading crowns and characteristic drooping branchlets. The foliage is grey-green, bark grey-brown and relatively smooth, sometimes breaking into small blocks. Spines are straight, paired, pale coloured and inconspicuous. Leaves are alternate, twice-pinnate. Mainly confined to the banks and beds of rivers and bigger spruits north of Shingwedzi; also a small number in the south near Crocodile Bridge and Lower Sabie.

The wood is off-white, without heartwood. It is easily worked; stems make good fence poles. Also used as firewood. Bark is used medicinally. Pods are highly regarded as fodder, eaten by a variety of wild animals.

1 Flowers (late summer–autumn) borne in elongated spikes, pale cream.
2 Pods (early summer) are orange to reddish brown, curled into a circular coil or variously twisted.

Sycamore fig

Ficus sycomorus subsp. *sycomorus*

A medium-sized to large evergreen to semi-deciduous tree. The main stem is relatively short, smooth and yellowish grey, sometimes with deep lengthwise folds. The crown is dense and very widely spreading. The bark peels off in paper-thin shreds. Leaves are alternate and simple, with milky latex. Occurs everywhere in the Park along rivers and rivulets with permanent water. In the high-rainfall Pretoriuskop area, also found in deep, sandy soils on the granite ridges.

The wood is pale brown, light and without heartwood. It is used as a general-purpose timber, also to make drums. Young leaves are cooked as a relish. Figs are consumed by birds and other animals. The bark and leaves are used medicinally.

1 Figs (all year round) reach up to ± 30 mm in diameter. **2** Fruit borne on large leafless clusters of branchlets, on the main stem and thicker branches.

Lala palm

Hyphaene coriacea

A small to medium-sized evergreen palm with an unbranched, cylindrical, fairly straight stem, suckering and forming clumps, and a relatively small crown. Leaves are fan-shaped, and dead ones hang down; leaf stalks with black spines along the edges. Occurs mainly on basaltic soils on the eastern side of the Park and south of the Olifants River; usually in low-lying areas, away from and close to water. Replaced by the similar-looking makalani palm (see following page) north of the Olifants River. The fruit shape differentiates the two.

Sap collected from stems is used to brew an alcoholic beverage. Leaves are used to weave items such as mats, baskets and hats. Seeds, known as vegetable ivory, are carved into ornaments and curios – a humane alternative to elephant ivory. It is heavily browsed by elephant. African Palm Swifts roost and nest in the skirt of dead leaves.

1 Flowers (late spring–early summer) in drooping clusters. **2, 3** Fruit (± 2 years to ripen) square or pear-shaped, 40–60 mm in diameter, dark brown, shiny, inedible.

Makalani palm
Hyphaene petersiana

A medium-sized to large evergreen palm with an unbranched, cylindrical, fairly straight stem, suckering and forming clumps, and a smallish crown. Leaves are fan-shaped, dead ones hang down; leaf stalks with black spines along edges. Occurs mainly near rivers in mopane veld; abundant north of the Letaba River. Replaced by the similar-looking lala palm (see previous page) south of the Olifants River. They can be told apart by their fruit shape.

Sap collected from stems is used to brew an alcoholic beverage. Leaves used to weave items such as mats, baskets and hats. Seeds, known as vegetable ivory, are carved into ornaments and curios – a humane alternative to elephant ivory. It is heavily browsed by elephant. African Palm Swifts roost and nest in the skirt of dead leaves.

1 Flowers (late spring–early summer) in drooping clusters. **2** Fruit (± 2 years to ripen) globose, 40–60 mm in diameter, dark brown, shiny.

117

Sausagetree
Kigelia africana

A medium-sized to large deciduous to semi-deciduous tree, shedding leaves in late winter or spring. The main stem is quite short, straight, relatively thick, and often grooved lengthwise. The crown is widely spreading and dense. Bark is grey-brown and fairly smooth, peeling off when very old in flat, irregular sections. Leaves are three-whorled, odd-pinnate. Distributed throughout the Park, but fairly rare. Usually grows on the banks of rivers and spruits. In the Pretoriuskop area it only occurs on higher ground.

The wood is pale brown and not very hard, but tough. It is used as a general-purpose timber. Roots yield a bright yellow dye. Leaves are consumed by elephant and kudu, flowers by nyala, and nectar by primates. Fruits are inedible and possibly poisonous, widely used in traditional medicine, and sometimes eaten by baboons and bushpigs. Seeds are edible after being roasted.

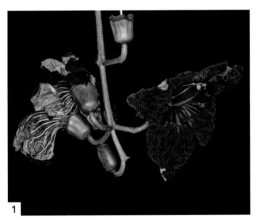

1 Flowers (spring) in drooping inflorescences, large, dark maroon with yellow venation. **2** Fruits (late summer–autumn) are sausage-shaped, very large (sometimes up to 500 mm long), hanging down on long, sturdy stalks.

Apple-leaf
Philenoptera violacea

A medium-sized to large deciduous to semi-deciduous tree that also grows as a shrub or small stunted tree. Leaves only fall in spring, over a short period of time. The main stem is rather long, crooked, and with twisted stems and branches. The crown is sparse to fairly dense and formless. Foliage is grey-green. Bark is fairly smooth and light grey, breaking up into small, flat blocks that peel off. Leaves are alternate and compound with three to five leaflets. Found on all soil types in the Park. The biggest specimens are confined to floodplains, and the banks of rivers and spruits. Beautiful specimens grow in Letaba Rest Camp.

Wood is yellowish, without heartwood, finely textured, hard and fairly heavy; often damaged by insects. Used to make traditional African mortars and implement handles. Roots and leaves used medicinally. Leaves eaten by browsers especially elephant. Butterflies that breed on the tree include the Large Blue Charaxes and the Striped Policeman.

1 Flowers (spring) in large branched inflorescences, mauve-purple, short-lived.
2 Pods (late summer) flat, hairless, single- or double-seeded. **3** Leaves usually greyish green, with developing pods almost the same colour.

121

Wild datepalm

Phoenix reclinata

A graceful evergreen palm with a slender, unbranched cylindrical stem. It almost always grows in dense clumps. Pendulous, spreading leaves form a crown, with the older drooping leaves and bases of shed leaves below. Occurs throughout the Park on the banks and in the beds of rivers and larger spruits. More abundant south of the Olifants River.

The fruit is edible and tasty, and consumed by birds, monkeys and baboons. Fallen fruit is eaten by nyala and bushbuck. Palm wine is brewed from the sap. Leaf fibres are used to make mats, baskets and hats, and brooms are made from frayed stems. Leaves and stems are browsed by elephant.

1 Flowers (spring) in cream to yellow sprays; male and female flowers occur on separate plants. **2** Fruit (summer–autumn) in drooping clusters only on female trees, maturing from yellow to brown.

Quininetree
Rauvolfia caffra

A medium-sized to large deciduous tree, sometimes evergreen in moist conditions. The main stem is long, bare and straight. The crown is widely spreading, round and fairly dense, with thinner branches and somewhat drooping foliage. Bark is soft and corky, breaking up into small, regular, elongated pieces. Leaves are in whorls of two to six, simple, with milky latex. Occurs throughout the Park next to rivers, springs and larger streams with permanent water. Most abundant in the Punda Maria and Pafuri area.

The wood is soft, light, grey to off-white and coarsely grained. It is easy to work with and has been used for furniture, household utensils, woodcuts and drums. Leaves, bark and roots contain various alkaloids and are widely used in traditional medicine (bark infusions famously used for treatment of malaria). The common name is a misnomer as the tree does not contain the alkaloid quinine. The ripe fruit is popular with vervet monkeys and fruit-eating birds.

1 Flowers (winter–spring) in terminal sprays, small, white. **2** Fruit (summer) fleshy, green with white spots, becoming black and wrinkled when ripe.
3 Leaves bright green, arranged in whorls, somewhat drooping.

Narrow-leaved mustardtree

Salvadora australis

A small to medium-sized evergreen tree with a very short, crooked and often grooved main stem. The crown is sparse, spreading, twiggy and formless, with branch tips drooping, often almost to the ground unless browsed. Foliage is greyish green. Bark is pale grey with dark blotches, shed as very small, irregular blocks. Leaves are opposite and simple. Limited to the eastern side of the Park (basalt) and only common along the Shingwedzi River (near the rest camp) and at Pafuri near the eastern boundary.

The wood is heavy, fairly hard, finely grained, and with a pale brown marbled appearance. Apparently it is not used at all. Leaves and roots are used in traditional medicine. The fruit is edible (not tasty) and popular with birds; also eaten by game and livestock but known to taint milk, giving it an unpleasant taste. Heavily browsed, especially by impala, kudu and elephant.

1 Flowers (winter–spring) in heads, tiny, greenish white. **2** Fruit (early summer) slightly fleshy, ± 5 mm in diameter, greenish pink.

Weeping boerbean
Schotia brachypetala

A medium-sized deciduous tree with a single main stem branching relatively low down; particularly attractive when in full flower. Leaves are shed over a short period in spring, with new ones appearing immediately afterwards. The crown is widely spreading, round to umbrella-shaped, and with drooping branch ends. Bark is rough and dark grey, breaking up into small, irregular blocks that peel off. Leaves are alternate and even-pinnate. Occurs fairly generally throughout the Park, but more abundant south of the Sabie River. The species invariably grows on termite mounds or on the banks of rivers and spruits.

The sapwood is yellow-grey and heartwood dark brown to black, finely grained, hard and quite heavy. It is excellent for manufacturing furniture, and also makes for good firewood. Bark and leaves are used medicinally, and the bark is also used for tanning and dyeing. Nectar drips from the flowers when a branch is shaken, and is consumed by baboons, monkeys, birds (especially sunbirds) and insects. In addition, watery excretions by the sap-sucking nymphs of spittlebugs cause the trees to 'rain' or 'weep' during certain times of the year. Seeds are edible after roasting.

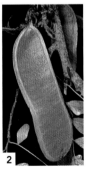

1 Flowers (spring) mainly in clusters on the old wood, deep red or scarlet.
2 Pods (late summer) flat and woody, splitting open while still on the tree.
3 Seeds pale brown with a yellow fleshy appendage (aril).

129

Tamboti
Spirostachys africana

A small to medium-sized deciduous tree, with leaves turning red to red-brown in autumn. The main stem is relatively long and straight; sometimes the tree is multi-stemmed. The crown is roughly round and relatively dense. Bark is almost black, breaking up into small, rectangular sections in a grid-like pattern. Leaves are alternate and simple, with milky latex. Widespread, but not on basalt plains or granite undulations. Abundant in the mopane woodland south of Punda Maria, the sandveld of Nwambiya (in low-lying areas) and especially on the brackish flats in the south, such as along the Lower Sabie road.

The wood is exceptional and well known, an excellent material for furniture. It is heavy and very hard. Sapwood is narrow and yellowish, heartwood is dark brown with paler and darker blotches. The timber contains a poisonous substance that causes severe eye irritation and the latex is poisonous, so the wood is not to be used for cooking, but it does make good firewood. Crushed stems are used in pools and rivers to stun fish. Seeds may be infested by larvae of a species of snout moth, which causes them to 'hop' around on the ground, especially on hot days.

1 Flowers (early spring) in spikes, very small, yellow and red. **2** Fruit (late spring) a three-lobed capsule, splitting into three segments. **3** Bark dark grey to blackish, cracked into a grid-like pattern of flakes.

Umdoni
Syzygium cordatum

A medium-sized evergreen tree with a short and often crooked main stem. The crown is dense, spreading and roundish. Young twigs are four-angled. Bark is nearly white to almost black, slightly rough, breaking up into irregular blocks and seldom peeling off. Leaves are opposite and simple. Occurs throughout the Park near permanent water and especially abundant in the Sabie River. In the Pretoriuskop area it also grows far from water.

Wood is brown with a reddish tinge, medium-hard and medium-heavy, and finely grained. It is exceptionally durable, especially in water, making it a good material for boat-building and jetty construction. Bark is used medicinally and as a fish poison. Flowers are rich in nectar and popular with insects. Fruit is eaten by primates, birds and bushpigs, and also fermented to produce beer. Leaves are not browsed by game, but this is a food plant for the larvae of various moths and butterflies.

1 Flowers (spring) in clusters at ends of branchlets, white to pinkish, fluffy.
2 Berries (late spring–summer) oval, deep purple to black when ripe.

Bushveld Natal-mahogany

Trichilia emetica subsp. *emetica*

A medium-sized to large evergreen tree with a low-branching main stem with vertical grooves. The crown is widely spreading, round and dense, with drooping branchlets and dark green foliage. Bark is fairly smooth and dark grey-brown. Leaves are alternate and odd-pinnate. This water-loving species is found along almost all rivers and larger spruits that have year-round water, except along the Shingwedzi River and its tributaries. In general it is rather rare, but it has been planted in most rest camps.

The wood is light brown with a red tinge, and without heartwood. It is fairly soft and light, suitable for manufacturing furniture and household utensils, and to carve curios. Bark is used in traditional medicine. Leaves are seldom browsed by game. The oil-rich seeds are used medicinally and to make soap, also eaten by birds. The red fleshy appendage (aril) of the seed is removed and cooked as a vegetable.

 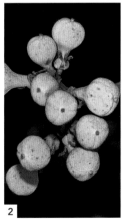 

1 Flowers (spring) in dense axillary clusters at the ends of branches, creamy green. **2** Fruit (summer) a pear-shaped capsule. **3** Seeds black, almost completely enveloped by a vivid orange fleshy appendage (aril).

Horned thorn
Vachellia grandicornuta

A small to medium-sized deciduous thorntree with a somewhat crooked and low-branching main stem. The crown is spreading and roundish to formless, with young branches growing in a zigzag fashion. Bark is dark grey with fairly deep vertical grooves. Spines are paired, straight, white, and up to 80 mm long. Leaves are alternate or in tufts, and twice-pinnate. Mainly confined to the brackish flats in the south of the Park, especially along the Sabie River, but also found in the north at Pafuri.

The wood is fairly heavy, hard, pale brown, and without heartwood. It is damaged by woodborers and evidently not used in any way. Leaves are consumed by browsers, and pods – particularly the seeds – by baboons and monkeys.

1 Flowers (irregular, spring–summer) in white balls. **2** Pods (autumn–winter) are flat, curved, hairless, yellowish brown when mature, splitting open while still on the tree.

Scented-pod
Vachellia nilotica subsp. *kraussiana*

A small to medium-sized deciduous thorntree with a short and somewhat crooked main stem. The crown is almost umbrella-shaped to rounded, with drooping branch ends. Bark is dark grey or black, with deep vertical grooves. Spines are paired and white, usually bending backward. Leaves are alternate or in tufts, and twice-pinnate. Occurs throughout the Park, but only on the low-lying brackish areas along spruits and rivers. Abundant in the southern areas. Seldom found in rocky situations or near year-round water.

The wood is hard and heavy. Sapwood is pale brown and heartwood is dark brown to red-brown. Timber is used for fencing posts and firewood. Bark exudes an edible gum, which is used in traditional medicine. Leaves are browsed by game. The pods are eaten by game and stock, but are said to be toxic to goats; also used to produce dyes.

1 Flowers (spring–summer) in golden-yellow balls. **2** Pods (winter) are flat, straight, black when mature, deeply constricted between the seeds, and do not split open.

Narrow-pod robust thorn
Vachellia robusta subsp. *clavigera*

A medium-sized to large deciduous thorntree with a medium-length to long main stem. The crown is widely spreading, round and dense. Foliage is exceptionally dark green. Bark is dark grey or black and develops shallow, lengthwise grooves. Spines are paired, straight and often under-developed. Leaves are borne on short woody cushions and are twice-pinnate. Occurs throughout the Park on the banks of rivers and spruits. Several specimens at Tshokwane.

The wood is fairly heavy, and pale yellow-brown to dark red. It is unsuitable for carpentry but used for making yokes. Inner bark fibre is used to make rope. Leaves are eaten by kudu and seldom by elephant.

1 Flowers (early spring) in creamy white balls. **2** Pods (late summer) are flat, slightly curved, 10–20 mm wide, splitting open while still on the tree.

Fevertree
Vachellia xanthophloea

A medium-sized deciduous thorntree with a relatively long and bare main stem. The crown is spreading, sparse and usually rounded. Bark is exceptionally smooth, yellowish green and powdery, sporadically peeling off in minute paper-thin flakes, or locally as larger dark brown or black scales. Spines are in pairs, straight and white. Leaves are borne in tufts and are twice-pinnate. This species only grows in the eastern half of the Park (basalt), in spruits and depressions, and next to rivers – it needs moist conditions. There is an impressive stand of trees at Pafuri.

The wood is pale brown, without heartwood, and fairly hard and heavy. It suffers severe damage by exceptionally large woodborers. Timber is suitable for furniture, carving and poles. Root and bark are used in traditional medicine. Pods, leaves, branches and gum are consumed by various wild animals; elephant may do extensive damage. The trees were once mistakenly thought to be the cause of malaria (hence the common name), because the malaria-carrying mosquito and the tree prefer the same habitat.

1 Flowers (spring) in bright yellow balls. **2** Pods (late summer) flat, straight and do not split open. **3** Bark unmistakable; smooth, yellowish green.

143

Nyalatree
Xanthocercis zambesiaca

A large evergreen to semi-deciduous tree with a short main stem, rarely multi-stemmed. Older trees have deep lengthwise folds. The crown is huge and dense, with drooping branches. Bark is dark grey and rough, and does not peel off. Leaves are alternate and odd-pinnate. Mainly confined to the alluvial soils next to rivers and spruits. Older trees often occur on massive termite mounds. A fairly rare tree, except in the Pafuri area, where several are found.

The wood is hard and heavy. Sapwood is off-white and heartwood is pale buff-brown. It is easy to work with but the sawdust may irritate the nose and throat. Used as a general-purpose timber. Fruits are eaten by birds, nyala (hence the common name) and various other game species, as well as humans (though it is not particularly tasty). Lowest branches are usually leafless due to browsing by animals such as kudu, impala and bushbuck.

1 Flowers (spring) in short sprays, white, inconspicuous. **2** Fruit (autumn–winter) fleshy, one- or two-seeded, yellowish brown when ripe. **3** Leaves dark glossy green above.

145

Pod-mahogany
Afzelia quanzensis

A large deciduous tree with a long bare trunk and a dense, widely spreading rounded crown with a flat top. The bark is smooth in youth, becoming dark grey with age and flaking off in thick round scales. Leaves are alternate and even-pinnate. Occurs on koppies, ridges and deep, sandy soil. Abundant in the Punda Maria area. Also found in the Nwambiya sandveld and the Lebombo range down to the Crocodile River. Some trees grow south of Orpen Gate and next to the Nhlanguleni road.

The wood is valuable, with heartwood reddish brown, strong and heavy. Pod-mahogany timber is traded as *chamfuta* or *chamfuti*. Bark and roots are used medicinally. The striking seeds are eaten by rodents and birds, and used for curios such as necklaces. A food source for elephant. Several species of *Charaxes* butterflies breed on the tree.

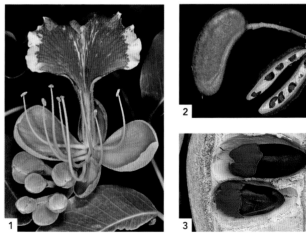

1 Flowers (spring) have a single large petal streaked with red. **2** Pods (autumn) are large, flat and woody, splitting open while on the tree. **3** Seeds are black with a scarlet fleshy covering (aril).

Large-leaved false-thorn
Albizia versicolor

An attractive medium-sized to large deciduous tree, with leaves turning yellow in autumn. The main trunk is long and bare; the crown spreading and roundish, almost umbrella-shaped. The bark is slightly rough, broken up into flat blocks. Leaves are alternate, twice-pinnate and dark reddish brown when young. Mainly in well-drained sandy soil in the Pretoriuskop area, as well as the sandveld of Punda Maria. Often grows along watercourses.

The wood is fairly soft and light with white sapwood and beige to red-brown heartwood. Resembling kiaat, it is excellent for the manufacture of furniture, drums and traditional African mortars. Bark was formerly used in poison for arrows. Roots and bark are used medicinally. Leaves are eaten by kudu and elephant. Pods (mainly unripe) are highly toxic to stock. Seeds are eaten by Brown-headed Parrots.

1 Flowers (late spring) in rounded fluffy heads, creamy white when receptive for pollination, yellowish when spent. **2** Pods (autumn–winter) are flat, glossy, brown to reddish brown.

Tasselberry

Antidesma venosum

A small to medium-sized, semi-deciduous to evergreen tree with a short, low-branching and sometimes crooked main stem. The dense crown is rounded, with drooping branch ends. Bark is pale grey and fibrous, with shallow vertical grooves. Leaves are alternate and simple. Fairly abundant in the deep, sandy soils of the Pretoriuskop and Punda Maria areas; also on the Lebombo range.

The wood is light and fairly soft, without heartwood. It is a pale buff-brown with a red tinge. Fruits are consumed by humans and are also popular with birds. Bark, root, leaves and fruits are used in traditional medicine. Leaves are seldom eaten by browsers.

1 Flowers (summer) in drooping spikes, very small, greenish yellow. **2** Berries (summer–autumn) globose, ± 8 mm in diameter, ripening from pale yellow-white to red, then purplish black. **3** Inflorescences are often parasitised by insects and transformed into large, tangled, sterile growths or galls.

151

Wild-seringa
Burkea africana

A medium-sized deciduous tree with a relatively tall main stem. The crown is spreading with a flat top, but is sometimes rounded. Bark is rough, subdivided into small blocks. Tips of the branchlets have velvety, reddish brown hairs. Leaves are alternate, twice-pinnate. Confined to the sandveld area around Punda Maria; can be seen along the Mahogany Loop and at Dzundzwini Hill.

The wood is hard and tough, medium-heavy. Sapwood is white and heartwood pale red to red-brown and durable, used for furniture, parquet floors and fencing posts. Bark is rich in tannin, and was formerly used for tanning and as a fish poison. Bark and roots are used in traditional medicine. Consumed by elephant, it is also a favourite food for the larvae of the Pallid Emperor Moth, which may cause complete defoliation of trees.

1 Flowers (spring) hang in drooping strings with the new leaves, small, white.
2 Pods (summer) flat, elliptic, wing-like, brownish, with a single seed.

Hornpod
Diplorhynchus condylocarpon

A small to medium-sized deciduous tree or shrub, mostly multi-stemmed. The crown is sparse and poorly spreading, with long, lax, drooping branchlets. Bark is fairly smooth and grey, sometimes breaking up and peeling off sporadically in small sections. Leaves are opposite and simple, containing milky latex. Limited to the sandveld areas around Punda Maria, where it is fairly common.

This wood is rather hard, medium-heavy, tough and pale brown, with a small, soft core. It is suitable for small carved ornaments. The latex is sticky and may be used as glue. Leaves and roots are used in traditional medicine. Elephant are partial to browsing the species.

1 Flowers (spring) are small, white and sweet-scented. **2** Fruit (late summer–autumn) is pod-like, arranged in widely spreading pairs, covered with numerous small whitish dots.

Mobolaplum
Parinari curatellifolia

A small to medium-sized evergreen or semi-deciduous tree with a usually bare main stem and a rounded crown with drooping branchlets. Foliage is dark green with a brownish tinge. Bark is corky, dark grey and grooved lengthwise. Leaves are alternate and simple. Occurs only on rather sour, well-drained, sandy soils in both the Pretoriuskop and Punda Maria areas.

Wood is pale brown, without heartwood, fairly heavy and difficult to work with because it contains silica crystals that rapidly blunt saw blades. Not durable, but may be used for general construction, poles and pounding blocks (tailor's tool). Bark and leaves are used in traditional medicine and tanning. Leaves seldom eaten by animals. Fruit has a pleasant taste and is eaten by a variety of wild animals; also fermented to make beer. The oil-rich nuts are edible and consumed by humans.

1 Flowers (spring) in axillary, hairy clusters, white, tinged pinkish. **2** Fruit (autumn–winter) is fleshy, 50 × 25 mm, brownish yellow and greyish scaly, usually ripening on the ground.

Camel's foot
Piliostigma thonningii

A small deciduous tree with a short and somewhat crooked main stem. The crown is spreading and rounded but often flattened on top, dense and with drooping branch ends. Bark is light grey to nearly black, splitting into lengthwise ridges but not deeply grooved. Leaves are alternate, simple and two-lobed (hence the common name). Occurs on sandy soil, only in the Pretoriuskop and Punda Maria areas, and also in a small area south of Orpen Rest Camp.

The wood is fairly light, without well-defined heartwood, but the colour deepens gradually from pale brown at the outer edge to dark brown in the centre. It is not generally used. The bark is rich in tannins and is used in traditional medicine. Pods, roots and seeds produce a black, dark blue or red-brown dye. Mature pods are ground into a flour consumed by humans, and green pods have been used as soap. Leaves and pods are a food source for elephant, kudu and baboons. It is also a larval food plant for the Bushveld Charaxes butterfly.

1 Flowers (summer) in axillary or terminal sprays, white or pinkish. **2** Pods (winter) are large, flat and woody, never splitting open.

Kiaat

Pterocarpus angolensis

A medium-sized to large deciduous tree with a long and straight main stem. The crown is widely spreading, flattened and fairly dense. Bark is dark grey to black, rough, and subdivided into irregular blocks loosely arranged in vertical rows. Leaves are alternate and odd-pinnate. Almost always associated with deep, sandy soils, it is readily found in the Pretoriuskop area, also in a limited area between Skukuza and Crocodile Bridge, on a stretch between Skukuza and Orpen, and in the Punda Maria vicinity.

Well known locally as a furniture wood, kiaat (wild teak) is fairly light with off-white sapwood and brown heartwood with lighter blotches; elsewhere in its range light brown to red or even copper-brown. Damaged bark exudes blood-red gum, which is used medicinally and as a dye. Roots are used for medicinal purposes and are also alleged to have magical properties. Leaves are eaten by kudu, and elephant push over and consume the trees. Pods are eaten by baboons and monkeys.

1 Flowers (spring) in branched inflorescences, orange-yellow. **2** Leaves with developing (green) and mature (brown) pods. **3** Pods (late summer) circular, with a central thickening densely covered by coarse bristles, surrounded by a broad wavy wing. **4** Bark dark grey, rough, cracked into almost rectangular blocks.

Black monkey-orange

Strychnos madagascariensis

A multi-stemmed shrub or small deciduous to semi-deciduous tree. The stem is short, fairly straight, and mostly grooved or dented. The crown is widely spreading, fairly dense and twiggy. Bark is pale grey and smooth. Leaves are opposite or in tufts, and simple. Occurs throughout the Park except on the basalt soils between the Lebombo Mountains (rhyolite) and the western half of the Park (granite) from the Crocodile River to the Limpopo River; more abundant and bigger in the Pretoriuskop area; shrubs often form dense stands in sandy soil.

The wood is fairly heavy, pale biscuit-coloured, blotched and very coarsely grained. It is used mainly for fuel. Fruit pulp is edible and sometimes smoked, dried and stored for later use. Seeds are considered to be poisonous; the plant contains strychnine-type alkaloids.

1 Flowers (spring) in clusters, greenish yellow, inconspicuous. **2** Fruit (all year) globose, 80–100 mm in diameter, orange when mature.

Silver clusterleaf
Terminalia sericea

A small to medium-sized deciduous tree with a short and fairly low-branching main stem. The crown is upright to spreading, sparse, and with a distinctive horizontal-branching habit that gives a layered appearance. Foliage is silvery grey, reflective in sunlight. Bark is pale to dark grey, subdividing lengthwise into wavy, undulating ridges. Leaves are simple, clustering towards ends of branches. Limited to deep, sandy soils in the western half of the Park (granite), the Soutpansberg sandstone of Punda Maria, Nwambiya and Pumbe sandveld areas, as well as on the Holkrans (Karoo) sandstone between the basalt (east) and granite (west). Especially abundant and dominant in the Pretoriuskop area.

Freshly cut wood is yellow. Dry wood is differentiated in dark, dirty-yellow sapwood and large, pale brown heartwood. The timber is fairly heavy and hard, making it suitable for furniture, and for building fences and huts. The bark yields an edible yellow-brown gum used as a dye; the fibres are used as rope in hut construction. Roots are widely used in traditional medicine. Leaves are consumed by domestic stock and game.

1 Flowers (spring–summer) in axillary spikes, small, pale cream to pale yellow.
2 Fruit (late summer–autumn) is flat, surrounded by a wing, pink to purplish red, drying to reddish brown.

Paperbark thorn

Vachellia sieberiana var. *woodii*

A medium-sized deciduous thorntree with a long, bare main stem and a spreading, flat-topped or rounded crown. Bark is dark yellow-grey, breaking up lengthwise and peeling off in flat and thin grey pieces, exposing yellowish layers underneath. Spines are paired, straight and white, often small and inconspicuous in mature growth. Leaves are alternate and twice-pinnate. Rare in the Park, mainly confined to the Pretoriuskop vicinity, and near Crocodile Bridge and the Nhlanguleni picnic spot. It prefers fairly wet conditions.

Wood is off-white with a yellow tinge and without heartwood. It is not durable and is seldom used. The inner bark yields a strong fibre traditionally used for stringing beads. An edible gum is exuded from damaged stems. Leaves and pods are browsed by game and livestock, although when wilted they are poisonous to livestock due to the presence of prussic acid.

1 Flowers (spring) in pale cream to white balls. **2** Pods (autumn–winter), thick, woody, almost straight, dirty yellow to pale brown.

Rock false-thorn
Albizia brevifolia

A medium-sized, slender deciduous tree. It tends to be multi-stemmed and has a very sparse formless crown, with long floppy bare branches. The bark is grey and rough, peeling off in thin blocks or strips. Leaves are alternate, twice-pinnate. Mainly limited to rocky places on basalt, sandstone and rhyolite north of the Olifants River, but there is a dense stand on Nwamuriwa Hill near Orpen Dam. Fairly abundant in the Pafuri area.

The wood is heavy, off-white, without heartwood, and is often damaged by borers. Hard-wearing, it is used for picks and axe handles. The bark is used in hut construction. Elephant and giraffe eat the leaves.

1 Flowers (spring) appear together with new leaves. Florets are small and white, with long, thin stamens. **2** Pods (autumn) hanging, pale brown, with fairly straight edges. Once shed, they are mostly twisted and split open.

Lebombo-ironwood
Androstachys johnsonii

A medium-sized to large evergreen tree. The main trunk tends to be long, bare and straight when trees grow in dense stands. The crown is generally upright, but in open stands it can be irregularly round and sparse with side branches fairly low down. Foliage is dark greyish green. The bark is greyish white to nearly black, with lengthwise grooves, resembling the bark of mopane. Leaves are opposite and simple. Found in the Lebombo range northwards from the Olifants River vicinity, as well as on ridges in the Punda Maria–Pafuri area. Mostly in very dense, nearly homogeneous stands, recognisable as dark grey-green patches in the landscape.

The sapwood is pale brown and the heartwood dark brown. This timber is very hard, heavy and tough, making it durable and also insect resistant. It is a good material for fencing posts and construction. Leaves are eaten by elephant and other browsers.

1 Flowers (spring) are inconspicuous and wind-pollinated, with male and female blossoms on different trees. **2** Fruit (summer) is a three-lobed capsule that splits into three segments.

171

Velvet bushwillow

Combretum molle

A small to medium-sized deciduous tree, with leaves turning yellow to red-brown in autumn. The main stem is relatively long and bare and the crown is fairly dense, but weakly spreading. Bark is grey-black, breaking up into very small, irregular blocks, which peel off as thin flakes. Leaves are opposite and simple. Confined to hills and ridges in the Pretoriuskop and Malelane areas, the Lebombo range and the sandveld in the vicinity of Punda Maria.

The wood is fairly hard, undifferentiated and dirty yellow. Durable, it is suitable for general carpentry, but seldom used. Leaves, bark and roots are used in traditional medicine. A red and yellow dye is obtained from the leaves and roots, respectively. It is browsed by game, and is also a larval food for the Guineafowl and Morant's Orange butterflies.

1 Flowers (spring) in axillary spikes, greenish yellow, appearing before or with the new leaves. **2** Fruit (autumn) four-winged, ± 15–20 × 15–20 mm, yellowish green, flushed with red, drying brown. **3** Bark grey-black, cracked into small irregular blocks.

Velvet-leaved corkwood

Commiphora mollis

A small to medium-sized deciduous tree with a short, straight and bare main stem. The crown is round, spreading and twiggy, with branchlet tips more or less drooping. Bark is whitish to dark grey, smooth or peeling off in irregular, roundish blocks. Leaves are alternate, odd-pinnate, often borne towards the tips of twigs, and contain cloudy latex. Occurs throughout the Park, but never common.

The wood is light, soft and dirty white, without heartwood. Traditionally used to carve household utensils. Occasionally browsed by game and cattle. Elephant dig up and eat the juicy roots.

1 Flowers (spring–summer) borne in axillary clusters, small and inconspicuous, yellowish to pinkish. **2** Fruit (late summer) fleshy, densely hairy, brownish green or reddish, containing a black seed partly covered by a red fleshy appendage (aril). **3** Bark whitish to dark grey, relatively smooth.

175

Broad-leaved coraltree

Erythrina latissima

A small to medium-sized deciduous tree with a relatively long, bare main stem. The crown is fairly dense, spreading and round, sometimes slightly flattened. The twigs are thick and woolly, armed with short, brown hook thorns. Bark is grey with a yellow or red-brown tinge and corky texture, sometimes deeply grooved lengthwise and with ridges cracked crosswise. Leaves are alternate and compound with three large leaflets (terminal one 60–300 × 70–320 mm). Confined to the koppies and ridges in the Pretoriuskop and Malelane areas.

The wood is off-white, without heartwood. It is soft, very light and coarsely grained, not utilised. Bark is used medicinally. The leaves and bark are eaten by elephant. This is an attractive ornamental tree for frost-free gardens.

 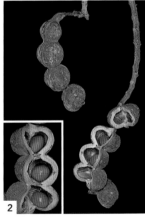

1 Flowers (spring) in sturdy heads, usually appearing before the new leaves, scarlet. **2** Pods (late summer–autumn) are cylindrical, woolly, and distinctively constricted at intervals; seeds ('lucky beans') are strikingly orange to red, with a black spot.

Common coraltree
Erythrina lysistemon

A distinctive small to medium-sized deciduous tree, with a usually low-branching main stem. The crown is spreading, roundish and fairly sparse. Young branchlets often have small, hooked spines. The bark is mostly smooth, irregularly and shallowly grooved lengthwise, sometimes peeling off in small blocks. Leaves are alternate, compound, with three leaflets. Only on koppies in the south (Pretoriuskop and Malelane) and on the sandstone ridges at Punda Maria. It has been planted in some rest camps.

The wood is without heartwood, yellowish to off-white, very soft and light. Leaves and bark are browsed by game. Flowers are popular with insects and birds. Seeds ('lucky beans') are used to make necklaces, but are poisonous when ingested. Various parts of the plant are used for medicinal and ritualistic purposes.

1 Flowers (spring) usually appear before the new leaves, bright red (rarely pink or white). **2** Pods (summer) are deeply constricted between the seeds, hairless; seeds are orange to red, with a black spot.

Bushveld candelabra-tree

Euphorbia cooperi var. *cooperi*

A succulent tree with a distinctive and idiosyncratic candelabra shape. It has one long and bare straight stem and a few dead branches below a dense crown of living, green branches at the top. Branches are shed with age, leaving noticeable round holes that appear to 'spiral' up the stem. Branches are usually five-angled with very prominent ridges, armed with thin grey spines when young. The bark is grey and rough. The tree produces milky latex. Occurs throughout the Park in stony areas, especially in the Lebombo and Olifants River regions.

The wood is white, light, soft and fibrous, devoured by termites when dry. The latex is poisonous and especially harmful when it comes into contact with eyes and skin. It releases volatile compounds that irritate the eyes and nose. It has been used in pools and rivers to stun fish. Seeds are eaten by birds.

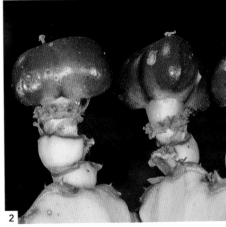

1 Flowers (spring) borne in clusters above the thorns, small, greenish yellow.
2 Fruit (spring–early summer) a three-lobed capsule, dull red to purplish.

181

Boekenhout
Faurea saligna

A small to medium-sized deciduous tree, with leaves turning reddish in autumn. The main stem is black or dark grey, the crown slender, upright and thinly spreading. The bark is very rough, deeply grooved lengthwise. Leaves are alternate, simple, and somewhat drooping. Confined mainly to sandy, granitic ridges and mountains in the Pretoriuskop and Malelane areas.

The wood is fairly heavy, pale to dark brown with an attractive net-like appearance. It is used for manufacturing the finest furniture and as a building material. It also makes excellent firewood. Bark was traditionally used for tanning leather. Various parts of the tree are used in traditional medicine.

1 Flowers (spring–summer) borne in hanging spikes, small, greenish to white.
2 Fruit (autumn) is a small nut covered with whitish hairs. **3** Bark rough, deeply fissured, dark grey-brown to almost black.

Large-leaved rock fig
Ficus abutilifolia

A small deciduous wild fig tree with a short, somewhat crooked main stem and a low-branching sparse crown. Bark is yellow-grey to yellow-white, peeling off in paper-thin flakes or thin, irregular blocks. Leaves are alternate, simple and relatively large (50–150 × 50–170 mm). The tree produces milky latex. Occurs throughout the Park on koppies and rocky ridges, but never abundant.

The wood is light and pale brown, not utilised. Leaves are used in traditional medicine. Fruits are eaten by wild animals; antelope favour the fallen fruit.

1 Fruit (all year) borne in the leaf axils towards tips of branchlets, 10–16 mm in diameter. **2** Fruit pale to dark red when ripe.

185

White-seringa

Kirkia acuminata

A medium-sized to large deciduous tree, with leaves turning bright yellow to red and red-brown in autumn. The main stem is long and straight, and the crown is widely spreading, mostly fairly flat-topped and rather sparse. Bark is pale grey, breaking up into small blocks that peel off. Leaves are alternate, odd-pinnate, and crowded towards the ends of branches. Occurs in Lebombo Mountains from near the Crocodile River to Pafuri, also on koppies in the western half of the Park from Roodewal Camp northwards. Especially abundant near Olifants Rest Camp and at Pafuri.

The wood is fairly light and soft. The sapwood is wide and off-white, heartwood is buff-brown. Timber is not durable or insect-proof. It is sometimes used to make furniture and household utensils. Inner bark is a source of fibre for making rope, but it is not durable. Roots are used medicinally and may be a source of water in an emergency. Sparsely consumed by game.

1 Flowers (late spring) in axillary, much-branched inflorescences, white or cream. **2** Fruit (autumn) is a dry, four-sided capsule, splitting into four one-seeded units. **3** Leaves become a vivid red in autumn.

187

Live-long
Lannea discolor

A small to medium-sized deciduous tree with a long, straight and bare main stem. The crown is neat and widely spreading, with greyish foliage. Twigs are exceptionally thick with prominent leaf scars. Bark is dark leaden-grey, slightly rough, and irregularly grooved lengthwise or cracked into small blocks that peel off. Leaves are alternate and odd-pinnate. Relatively rare in the Park, but prominent on granite in the vicinity of Pretoriuskop. Also occurs in the Lebombo range as well as the sandveld areas around Punda Maria.

The wood is soft, light, pale brown and coarse in texture. It is suitable for making stamping blocks, plates and spoons. Leaves, roots and bark are used in traditional medicine. The bark contains a strong fibre that is plaited into ropes. Fruit is edible, but skin must be discarded; consumed by humans and wildlife. Leaves are popular with browsers.

1 Flowers (spring) in spike-like inflorescences before the new leaves appear, small, creamy yellow, male and female on different trees (male illustrated).
2 Fruit (summer) fleshy, slightly flattened, reddish to purple-black when ripe.
3 Leaves dark green above, white-grey below.

189

Kuduberry

Pseudolachnostylis maprouneifolia

A medium-sized deciduous tree, with leaves turning dark red or yellow in autumn. The main stem is long and may be slightly bent. The crown is dense, round, and the lowest branches nearly reach the ground. Bark is pale grey to grey, cracking and later peeling off in small, irregular and rather thick sections. Leaves are alternate and simple. Found almost exclusively in stony areas, mostly on the Lebombo range northwards from the Olifants River, as well as on koppies and ridges in the Punda Maria area. There are a few specimens in the Letaba and Phalaborwa areas.

The wood is pale brown with darker rings, medium-heavy and medium-hard. It has a pungent odour. Roots and bark are used in traditional medicine. Leaves and fruit are eaten by duiker, kudu (hence the common name) and elephant. An infusion of the bark and leaves is used to wash traps set for kudu and other antelope.

1 Flowers (spring) in axillary clusters, small, greenish white. **2** Fruit (autumn–spring) is fleshy, spherical, yellowish brown, dotted with tiny white spots.

191

Glossary

Numbers in square brackets refer to the line drawings on page 195. Synonyms commonly used in botanical works are supplied for some terms and are given in round brackets at the end of the definition.

alternate see illustration [8].

aril a fleshy outer covering or appendage that encloses the whole or part of the seed, and usually develops from its stalk; often brightly coloured, it is consumed by birds, thus assisting in seed dispersal.

axil upper angle between the leaf and the stem on which it is carried; see illustration [2].

axillary bud see illustration [1].

basalt an extrusive (erupted and cooled at the Earth's surface) volcanic rock composed mainly of calcium-rich feldspar and pyroxene. On weathering, it gives rise to dark-coloured and fertile clay- or silt-rich soils.

berry a many-seeded fleshy fruit with a soft outer portion, with the seeds embedded in the fleshy or pulpy tissue (e.g. the tomato).

bilobed divided into two lobes; see illustration [2].

browser a plant-eating animal that specialises in eating leaves, soft shoots and fruits of high-growing woody plants as well as shrubs. A grazer eats mainly grass and other herbaceous plants.

capsule a dry fruit produced by an ovary comprising two or more united carpels and usually opening by slits or pores. Compare **pod**.

compound see illustrations [3–7].

deciduous refers to a plant that loses all its leaves for part of the year, usually at the end of the growing season. Compare **evergreen, semi-deciduous**.

dolerite a fine-grained intrusive (when molten rock emplaces into the Earth's crust and solidifies beneath the surface) igneous rock, usually occurring as dykes or sills, mineralogically equivalent to a basalt. On weathering, gives rise to reddish and fertile clayey soils. Compare **basalt**.

even-pinnate see illustration [6] (= paripinnate).

evergreen refers to a plant that retains green leaves throughout the year, even during the winter months. Compare **deciduous, semi-deciduous**.

florets small individual flowers that make up a (dense) inflorescence, as those in thorntrees.

fruit the ripened ovary (pistil) and its attached parts; the seed-containing structure. Compare **seed**.

gabbro a dark-coloured basic intrusive (when molten rock emplaces into the Earth's crust and solidifies beneath the surface) rock composed mainly of plagioclase feldspar and clino-pyroxene; basalt is a finer-grained extrusive equivalent. Gives rise to reddish and fertile clay-rich soils. Compare **dolerite**.

granite a coarse-grained, generally light-coloured intrusive (when molten rock emplaces into the Earth's crust and solidifies beneath the surface) igneous rock composed of quartz, feldspar, and some dark minerals such as biotite or amphibole. On weathering, it gives rise to nutrient-poor, coarse-grained, sandy soils.

heartwood wood in the centre of older stems that no longer conducts water and in which certain substances have accumulated; generally darker coloured than the functioning sapwood (= duramen). Compare **sapwood**.

inflorescence any arrangement of more than one flower; the flowering portion of a plant, e.g. head, spike.

koppie a South African term for a small but prominent, isolated rocky hill, frequently an erosion remnant (= inselberg, kopje).

latex liquid exudate released when a leaf is broken or tissue is damaged; it may be clear, cloudy, milky, or any colour.

leaf see illustrations [1, 2].

leaflet see illustrations [3–7] (= pinna, pinnule).

odd-pinnate see illustration [5] (= imparipinnate).

opposite see illustration [9].

palmately compound see illustration [4].

pinnately compound see illustrations [5, 6].

Umbrella thorn in full bloom, with termite mound.

pod a general term applied to any dry and many-seeded dehiscent (opening) fruit, formed from one unit or carpel. In this book the word is usually applied to a legume which is the product of a single pistil (carpel) and which usually splits open along one or both of the two opposite sutures or seams (a characteristic of many thorn- and false-thorn trees). Compare **capsule**.

quartzite a metamorphic rock consisting mainly of quartz, formed by the recrystallisation of sandstone. Gives rise to nutrient-poor, sandy soils. Compare **sandstone**.

rhyolite a type of volcanic rock, the extrusive equivalent of granite. Extremely resistant to weathering and associated soils tend to be shallow and rocky. Compare **granite**.

sandstone a sedimentary rock consisting of sand-sized quartz grains cemented together by either silica or carbonate, or clay minerals. On weathering gives rise to nutrient-poor sandy soils. Compare **quartzite**.

sapwood outer part of the wood in older stems containing cells still conducting water; generally lighter coloured than the heartwood (= alburnum). Compare **heartwood**.

seed the ripened ovule containing an embryo; borne in a fruit. Compare **fruit**.

semi-deciduous refers to a plant that loses its foliage for a short period, when old leaves fall off and new foliage growth begins; also when a plant loses some, but not all, of its leaves for part of the year, usually at the end of the growing season (= semi-evergreen). Compare **deciduous, evergreen**.

shale a fine-grained sedimentary rock formed by the consolidation of silt or mud. On weathering gives rise to nutrient-rich clayey soils.

simple see illustrations [1, 2].

skirt used in some tall-stemmed palms to refer to the thick layer of persistent, densely packed, dead leaves that fall against the trunk below the canopy of green leaves.

spike an inflorescence with stalkless flowers arranged along an elongated, unbranched axis.

spray a slender shoot or branch together with its leaves, flowers or fruit.

spruit a South African term for a small watercourse, typically dry except during the rainy season.

suckering producing shoots that arise from below ground (suckers) from the roots some distance away from the main stem; resulting over time in what appears to be a clump of trees.

tufted see illustration [11] (= fascicled, clustered).

twice-pinnate see illustration [7] (= bipinnate, bipinnately compound).

valve one of the segments produced by the splitting of a dry fruit (e.g. pod or capsule) when ripe, thus separating from other such segments.

whorled see illustration [10] (= verticillate).

SIMPLE AND COMPOUND LEAVES

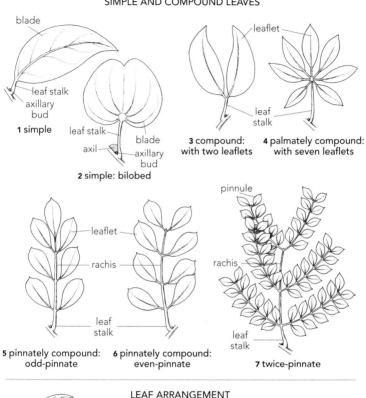

blade

leaf stalk
axillary bud

1 simple

leaf stalk

blade
axil
axillary bud

2 simple: bilobed

leaflet

leaf stalk

3 compound: with two leaflets

4 palmately compound: with seven leaflets

leaflet

rachis

leaf stalk

5 pinnately compound: odd-pinnate

6 pinnately compound: even-pinnate

pinnule

rachis

leaf stalk

7 twice-pinnate

LEAF ARRANGEMENT

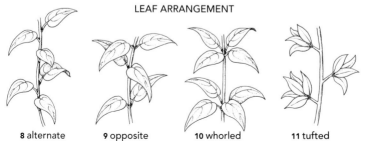

8 alternate

9 opposite

10 whorled

11 tufted

Bibliography

Boon, R. 2010. *Pooley's Trees of Eastern South Africa*, 2nd edition. Flora & Fauna Publications Trust, Durban.

Coates Palgrave, M. 2005. *Keith Coates Palgrave Trees of Southern Africa*, 3rd edition. Struik Publishers, Cape Town.

Codd, L.E.W. 1951. *Trees and Shrubs of the Kruger National Park. Botanical Survey Memoir 26*, Department of Agriculture, Union of South Africa, Pretoria.

Funston, M. 1993. *Bushveld Trees, Lifeblood of the Transvaal Lowveld* (text by Borchert, P. & Van Wyk, B.). Fernwood Press, Vlaeberg.

Gertenbach, W.P.D. 1983. Landscapes of the Kruger National Park. *Koedoe* 26: 9–122.

Grant, R. & Thomas, V. 2007. *Sappi Tree Spotting, Lowveld, including Kruger National Park*. Jacana Media, Johannesburg.

Greeff, M. 2017. *A Site-by-site Guide to Trees in the Kruger National Park*. Briza Publications, Pretoria.

Schmidt, E., Lötter, M. & McCleland, W. 2019. *Trees and Shrubs of Mpumalanga and Kruger National Park*, 2nd edition (updated). Jacana Media, Johannesburg.

Scholes, R.J. & Walker, B.H. 1993. *An African Savanna: Synthesis of the Nylsvley Study*. Cambridge University Press, New York.

Van Wyk, B. & Van Wyk, P. 2013. *Field Guide to the Trees of Southern Africa*, 2nd edition. Struik Nature, Cape Town.

Van Wyk, B. & Van Wyk, P. 2019. *How to Identify Trees in Southern Africa*, 2nd edition. Struik Nature, Cape Town.

Van Wyk, B., Van Wyk, P. & Van Wyk, B-E. 2008. *Photo Guide to Trees of Southern Africa*, 2nd edition. Briza Publications, Pretoria.

Van Wyk, P. 1972. *Trees of the Kruger National Park*, 2 vols. Purnell, Johannesburg.

Van Wyk, P. 2008. *Field Guide to the Trees of the Kruger National Park*, 5th edition. Struik Publishers, Cape Town.

Venter, F., Venter, J-A. & Joffe, P. 2015. *Making the Most of Indigenous Trees*, 3rd edition. Briza Publications, Pretoria.

Viljoen, M. 2015. The Kruger National Park: geology and geomorphology of the wilderness. In S. Grab & J. Knight (eds), *Landscapes and Landforms of South Africa*: 111–120. Springer, Cham, Switzerland.

Acknowledgements

I would like to convey my sincere thanks to all those who made it possible for this book to be produced. I am much indebted to Chenay Simms, SANParks Scientific Services, Kruger National Park, for GIS data used in the preparation of the maps. A special word of thanks to cartographers Nicholas De Kock and Lourens Snyman who constructed the maps used in this book; both are from the Geospatial Information Services unit, Department of Geography, Geoinformatics and Meteorology, University of Pretoria. For the line drawings used in the glossary, my grateful thanks go to Daleen Roodt. I am also much indebted to Elsa van Wyk for technical assistance.

I am much obliged to Emmarentia van Wyk, widow of Piet van Wyk (1931–2006), for help with the preparation of this book, and for permission to use some of Piet's tree photographs. I am also very grateful to the following individuals who kindly allowed the use of their photographs: Richard Boon, Wayne Matthews, Geoff Nichols, Marius Swart, Warwick Tarboton, Steven Whitfield and Joan Young. A word of gratitude to Christo Reitz (Briza Publications) for scans of images and also to those photographers who made images available for downloading via Wikimedia Commons.

Generous financial assistance that enabled some of Piet van Wyk's fieldwork on trees was received from principal sponsors Total SA (Pty) Ltd (fuel), Mazda Wildlife Fund (transport) and Agfa (film). Financial and institutional support was also provided by the South African National Research Foundation and the University of Pretoria.

Many thanks and much appreciation are due to the team at Struik Nature who worked with me on this publication, in particular Pippa Parker (Publisher), who conceptualised the book and commissioned the manuscript, Natalie Bell (Editor) and Gillian Black (Designer). My gratitude also to Emsie du Plessis who did the final proofreading.

Braam van Wyk

Photographic credits

Front cover: © Beate – SA
Back cover l: © javarman – SA;
 tr: Joan Young
Contents tl: © Jurgens – SA;
 tr: © Estela – SA; **ml:** © Amanda
 – SA; **br:** © Leonardo – SA
4: © Gallas – SA
5: Marius Swart – clearlyafrica.com
6: © Fokke Baarssen – SA
7: Steven Whitfield
8: © Jurgens – SA
20: © hpbfotos – SA
23: © Karlos Lomsky – SA
24: © Estela – SA
27: Braam van Wyk
30–31: © Willem – SA
33: tl: Braam van Wyk;
 tr: Joan Young
35 l: SAplants, CC BY-SA 4.0, WC;
 r: JMK, WC
37 l: SAplants, CC BY-SA 4.0, WC
39 tr: Joan Young
41 l: Braam van Wyk;
 m and r: Joan Young
43 l: Braam van Wyk
45 l: SAplants, CC BY-SA 4.0, WC;
 r: Bernard DUPONT from France,
 CC BY-SA 2.0, WC
47 l and m: SAplants, CC BY-SA
 4.0, WC; **r:** Joan Young
49 both: Braam van Wyk
51 both: Braam van Wyk
53 m and r: Braam van Wyk
55 r: Braam van Wyk
57 both: SAplants, CC BY-SA
 4.0, WC
59 both: Joan Young
61 both: Braam van Wyk
63 l: Braam van Wyk

65 r: Braam van Wyk
67 l: Braam van Wyk
69 l and r: Braam van Wyk;
 inset: JMK, WC
71 both: Joan Young
73 l: JMK, WC
75 all: Braam van Wyk
78 l: JMK, WC
79 tl and r: SAplants, CC BY-SA
 4.0, WC
83 l: Braam van Wyk; **r:** Hans
 Hillewaert, CC BY-SA 3.0, WC
85 both: Braam van Wyk
87 r: JMK, WC
89 l: JMK, WC; **insert
 and r:** Richard Boon
91 both: SAplants, CC BY-SA
 4.0, WC
93 l and br: SAplants, CC BY-SA
 4.0, WC; **tr:** JMK, WC
95 l: Braam van Wyk;
 m, inset and r: Joan Young
97 r: Joan Young
99 both: Braam van Wyk
101 m: Joan Young
103 tl: Braam van Wyk;
 r: Joan Young
105 all: Braam van Wyk
109 l and m: Braam van Wyk;
 r: Geoff Nichols
113 r: Braam van Wyk
115 l: Bernard DUPONT from
 France, CC BY-SA 2.0, WC;
 tr: Joan Young;
 br: Braam van Wyk
117 both: Bernard DUPONT from
 France, CC BY-SA 2.0, WC
119 l: Braam van Wyk; **r:** Landau,
 WC; **inset:** Joan Young
121 l and m: Braam van Wyk;
 r: Bernard DUPONT from
 France, CC BY-SA 2.0, WC
123 all: Braam van Wyk
125 l and r: Joan Young;
 m: SAplants, CC BY-SA 4.0, WC
127 both: Richard Boon
129 l and m: SAplants, CC BY-
 SA 4.0, WC; **r:** JMK, WC

131 l and m: Braam van Wyk
133 both: Braam van Wyk
135 l and m: Braam van Wyk;
 r: Joan Young
137 l: Bernard DUPONT from
 France, CC BY-SA 2.0, WC
139 l: SAplants, CC BY-SA 4.0,
 WC; **r:** Joan Young
141 r: SAplants, CC BY-SA
 4.0, WC
143 l and r: SAplants, CC BY-SA
 4.0, WC
145 l: Braam van Wyk; **tr** and
 br: Bernard DUPONT from
 France, CC BY-SA 2.0, WC
147 l: SAplants, CC BY-SA 4.0,
 WC; **br:** Joan Young
151 all: Braam van Wyk
153 both: SAplants, CC BY-SA
 4.0, WC
155 l: Braam van Wyk;
 r: Joan Young
157 l: Braam van Wyk; **br:** Hans
 Hillewaert, CC BY-SA 3.0, WC
161 l, mt and mb: SAplants, CC
 BY-SA 4.0, WC; **r:** Joan Young
163 l: Wayne Matthews; **tr:** Joan
 Young; **br:** Braam van Wyk
165 l: Braam van Wyk;
 r: Bernard DUPONT from
 France, CC BY-SA 2.0, WC
167 l: JMK, WC; **r:** SAplants, CC
 BY-SA 4.0, WC
171 l and r: Braam van Wyk
173 l and br: Braam van Wyk
175 br: Braam van Wyk
177 all: SAplants, CC BY-SA
 4.0, WC
179 both: SAplants, CC BY-SA
 4.0, WC
181 both: Braam van Wyk
183 l and m: SAplants, CC BY-
 SA 4.0, WC; **r:** Braam van Wyk
185 l: Braam van Wyk
187 l and r: Braam van Wyk
189 all: Braam van Wyk
191 l: Warwick Tarboton;
 r: Braam van Wyk

Index

Scientific names are in italics. Older scientific names (synonyms) are redirected to currently accepted names.

Pod-mahogany in Kruger.